UF…

THE SC… …IMENSION

RON HALLIDAY

Scottish Paranormal Press

Halliday, R
UFOs: The Scottish Dimension
I. Title

ISBN 0 9530795 0 3

Cover Design by Brian Maddison
Typeset by Leanne Hogg

First published in 1997 by
Scottish Paranormal Press
4 Linden Avenue
Stirling FK7 7PG

Printed at the University of Stirling

To my wife and best friend,

EVELYN

INTRODUCTION

Unlike some investigators, I would not claim that the subject of unidentified flying objects always fascinated me. On the contrary, for many years they did not interest me at all. Warminster and other UFO 'hot spots' passed me by completely. Objects from other planets? I, like many others, did not take it too seriously. I enjoyed science fiction, but did not see UFOs as something having an objective reality. When I look back, I find my attitude rather puzzling. I had from early times been fascinated by ghosts and all the paraphernalia of folk lore and folk stories. Tiny Miss Jones at Garth Primary School in Bangor (North Wales) was a story teller of genius and the tales she told of Bethgellert, the hound of Llwelleyn, Prince of Wales, still rings in my memory today. My father, a scientist, had an interest in psychical research and books he owned like *The Haunting of Borley Rectory* and *Psychical Research Today* made terrifying night time reading. It was while in later life researching a book on Scottish witchcraft cases that, for some unknown reason, a link between areas where many witchcraft cases were reported and UFO sightings crossed my mind. I was interested enough to contact BUFORA, who put me in touch with their representative in Scotland, Steuart Campbell. Steuart did not think much of my suggested link, but, because I was moving house, put me in touch with another UFO investigator, Malcolm Robinson. As it turned out, Malcolm was interested in everything I was, plus UFOs. As we began to carry out joint investigations I came into contact with individuals who had been through all kinds of experiences including seeing or having close encounters with UFOs. It began to dawn on me that many of these experiences could be classified within the general term 'paranormal'. It also seemed to me that UFOs as extraterrestrial phenomena was only one possible explanation. There were clearly similarities between UFO encounters and age old spiritual experiences and even ghosts, although superficially they might seem a world apart. My interest in the paranormal now developed hand-in-hand with my more specific involvement with ufology. What had at one time seemed like a not-too-likely UFO report now became fascinating as I compared sightings of a similar nature or researched the history of such reports from a defined area. Cases of close encounters or of alleged abductions took on a terrible significance as I began to grapple with the implications they posed for Man's position in the Cosmos. These cases, in particular, must be taken seriously as they do challenge our accepted view of the Universe.

The majority of cases included in this book were personally researched by me, some in conjunction with other colleagues from Scottish Earth Mysteries Research (SEMR) and others with the assistance of Kenny Higgins, then director of Scottish Research into Unidentified Flying Objects (SRUFO). SEMR has a substantial database of UFO reports, covering several hundred cases, and it is from this database that the bulk of these cases are drawn. There are, of course, exceptions. The Bob Taylor case of 1979 occurred several years before SEMR was formed, but has been included because of its world significance and the impact it had on the development of Scottish ufology. In addition, SEMR has investigated further UFO incidents associated with Mr Taylor's sighting which have only emerged in the last few years. Reference has also been made to the controversial Fife alien encounter case and the alleged abduction incident on the A70. These events received considerable publicity and, therefore, have been referred to in the general context of abductions. The 'Bonnybridge Triangle' is discussed in both general and specific terms.

UFOs: The Scottish Dimension includes much new material and case incidents which have not been previously discussed. I hope that this book, published on the fiftieth anniversary of Kenneth Arnold's epoch making sighting, will make a serious and full contribution to the development of ufology in Scotland.

Ron Halliday
Bridge of Allan
August 1997

ACKNOWLEDGMENTS

A list of acknowledgments can sometimes appear simply as an endless run of names. However, no piece of writing is ever produced without contributions intentionally or unintentionally made by many others, even if they disagree with the end result. I would like to thank the following for helping me on the path to the production of *UFOs: The Scottish Dimension*. I would particularly like to thank Viv Alexander, editor of *Phenomenal News* for her editorial contribution, her suggestions on material and layout and her written contribution to Chapter Eight. (The title is her fault, as well.) I would also thank Malcolm Robinson, Ken Higgins, Brian Wilson, Keith Mavor, Andrew McMichael, Brian Maddison and John Morrison. A special thanks is due to the early pioneers of Scottish ufology, John Sparks and W. P. Davidson. There is, of course, the wider world and a variety of well known writers such as Jenny Randles and Paul Devereux who have made many insightful comments which have focused my thoughts on specific areas. The media is often seen as a whipping boy, but I think that ufology in Scotland has undoubtedly benefited from their interest. I would also thank my father, Dr R Halliday, for first having inspired (if that's the right word!) my interest in the paranormal. Above all, I would thank my wife, Evelyn, for her tolerance over many years in allowing me without complaint to investigate the paranormal and work on this book. Last, but certainly not least, I would thank all the witnesses who have been prepared to stand up, risking ridicule, and tell of their personal encounter with the world of the unknown. Some have preferred not to reveal their names for the moment, a request I have unhesitatingly complied with.

CONTENTS

Significant Events in Scottish Ufology

1947 First confirmed Scottish UFO report as 'craft' seen in the Portobello district of Edinburgh (although there is evidence of a mysterious disc reported as early as 1937).

1952 Earliest UFO sighting in Glasgow.
Disc shaped object reported over Glasgow school.

1954 'Cedric Allingham' reports close encounter incident near Lossiemouth.

1956 East Lothian UFO 'wave'. First Scottish 'wave'. .Earliest UFO groups active in Scotland based in Edinburgh and East Lothian.

1958 Contactee George Adamski visits Scotland and speaks to packed halls.

1973 Christine alien entities and missing time incident in Fife.

1976 First incident in Karen abduction case, Tayside.

1979 SPI formed by Malcolm Robinson.
Bob Taylor incident - first Scottish UFO incident to receive world wide publicity.

1983 Tom Coventry's close up sighting of flying 'carriage'. Details not made public for several years.

1990 SEMR formed by Ron Halliday.
Plaque erected at site of Bob Taylor incident by Livingston Development Corporation.
UFO reported over Forth Bridge during centenary celebration.
Blairgowrie labelled UFO capital of Scotland.

1992 First Bonnybridge incident reported - start of UFO 'wave'.
A70 abduction case. Under hypnosis Gary Wood and Colin Wright describe abduction by alien entities.
Pat Macleod close encounter with Saturn-like object. Witness in area sees 'Mothman' - only such reported case in Scotland.

1996 Year of video footage.
Margaret Ross video footage, Stenhousemuir.
Barry McDonald video footage over Falkirk.
Both videos receive extensive publicity.
The McDonald video goes worldwide.
Isle of Lewis mystery explosion.

1997 Close encounter and missing time case, Cumbernauld.
'Multi aliens' case reported in Fife.

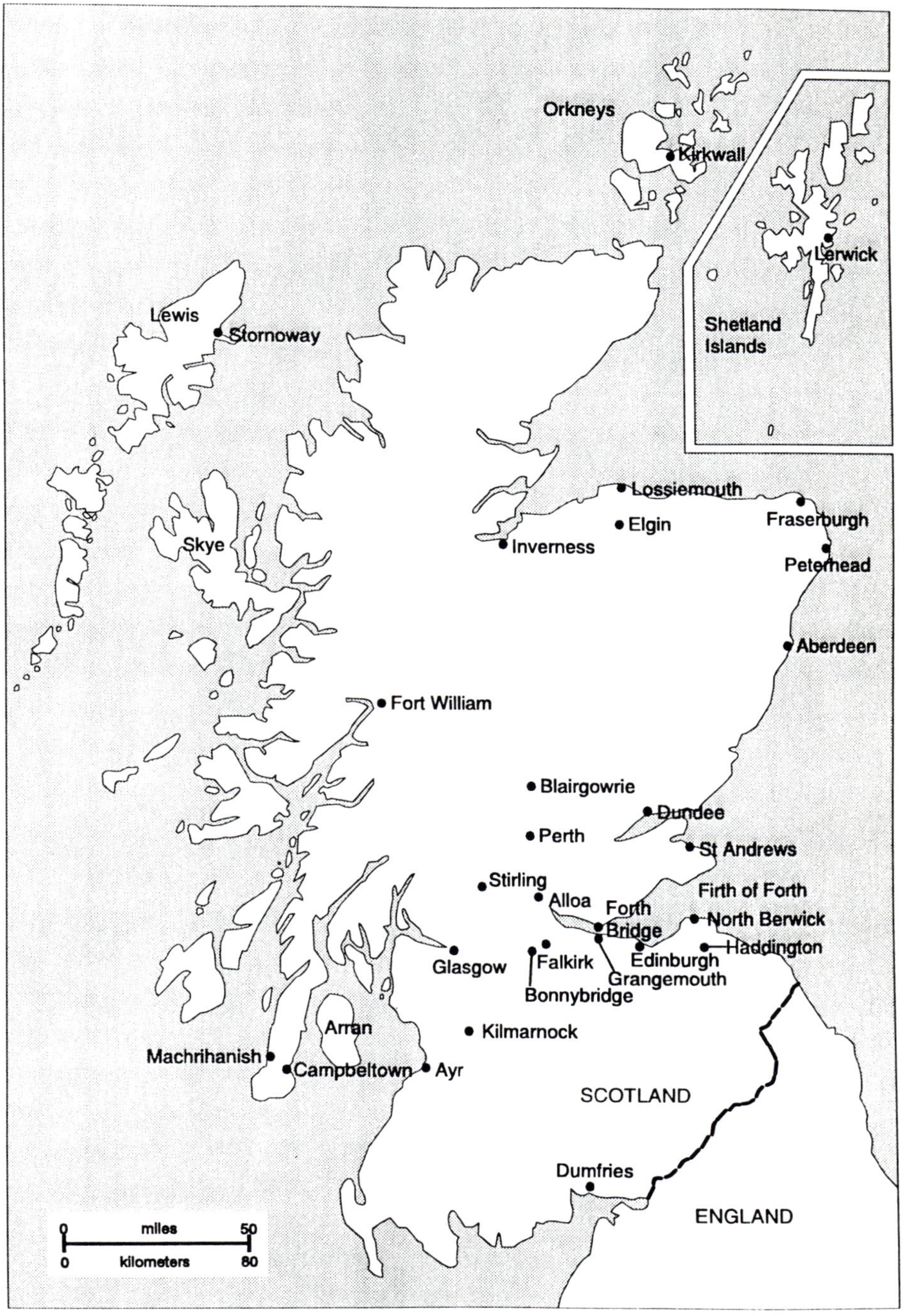
Orkneys
Kirkwall
Lerwick
Shetland Islands
Lewis
Stornoway
Lossiemouth
Fraserburgh
Elgin
Skye
Inverness
Peterhead
Aberdeen
Fort William
Blairgowrie
Dundee
Perth
St Andrews
Stirling
Firth of Forth
Alloa
Forth Bridge
North Berwick
Haddington
Glasgow
Falkirk
Edinburgh
Grangemouth
Bonnybridge
Arran
Kilmarnock
Machrihanish
Campbeltown
Ayr
SCOTLAND
Dumfries
ENGLAND
0 miles 50
0 kilometers 80

ONE

WAY UP OVER THE LOTHIANS

The Lothians, that broad swathe of country bordering the Firth of Forth, have long been famous in the annals of Scotland's history. It is not surprising, then, to find Edinburgh, Scotland's thriving capital of half a million souls, occupying the heart of Midlothian and acting as focus for the adjacent counties of West and East Lothian. It may astonish many to learn, however, that this rather traditional and comfortable city with its outlying landmarks is the centre, and has been for many years, of intense UFO activity.

Is there any obvious explanation for this phenomenon? On the whole, the land is mainly agricultural, with a decaying mining tradition, small scale industry, 'sunrise' technology factories, a vibrant financial centre and a variety of government departments. A picture which could be repeated in many different parts of Europe. Hardly one to excite the interest of alien spacecraft, you might think!

On the other hand, it is true that there are many army bases in the area, naval dockyards, defence personnel, nuclear bunkers and military aircraft activity. Is this what interests the ufonauts (if there is, indeed, intelligence behind their activities)? That UFOs had a particular interest in our defence capabilities used to be a standard view. However, the appearance of UFOs to a variety of people, in different circumstances, makes that increasingly unlikely as an explanation. Whatever the truth, there can be no doubt that something strange has been going on for decades both over the densely populated capital and around the scattered communities of West and East Lothian.

Mrs La Barre (42) a medical technical officer from Edinburgh was driving near Penicuik at 5.15 p.m. on 8 November 1992 when she spotted something out of the ordinary in the sky. She described it as 'a large, red light hovering ... over the Edinburgh area'. She, with her husband and daughter, Emily, watched it closely for two minutes when 'a part of it separated from the main bulk and went slowly towards the ground'. The object then vanished. No one reported the mysterious sphere landing, so it must have come down unobserved in some quiet spot, for who knows what purpose.

On 25 February 1996 Radio Forth broadcaster Tom Wilson was travelling east on the M8 motorway towards the outskirts of Edinburgh. As he approached the Harthill Services area, a bright orange ball appeared from nowhere and seemed to hover in the air. Having caught his attention, it then shot off at incredible speed, to be replaced by a second ball of identical colour which followed the first, both orange phenomena heading south. It was 10.05 p.m. and the glowing lights could be clearly seen against the scattered clouds of a dry, cold night. Both objects were large and must have stood out bigger than a full moon.

UFOs of all descriptions have been reported over this part of Scotland. Yet though daylight sightings of solo UFOs are few and far between, Lothian encounters are spectacular, and world renowned. Take, for example, the classic incident at Dechmont Law near Livingston.

November 9 1979 dawned cold and clear. The 3 a.m. edition of *The Scotsman* newspaper led on the furore over an 'IRA Stunt'. Jim Callaghan, the then Prime Minister, had condemned the BBC for allegedly filming an IRA propaganda exercise in Northern Ireland. The untimely death of Charles De Gaulle's widow was also announced.

On an inside page, columnist Albert Morris penned a feature 'Reflections of an Alien Kind'. In the article he discussed the attitude of extraterrestrials to an encounter with earthlings and wrote, 'It is not space monsters we have to fear ... but mankind itself'. It was almost as if the journalist had foreseen the astonishing event that was to take place that very morning. The object that was to cause such controversy might well have been that first seen at 8.05 a.m. A driver, Graham Kennedy, heading west on the A89, was passing Bangour Hospital when he noticed a bright light above and to the left of his car. It came fast towards him a few metres above the ground, on a collision course. Swerving to avoid a crash with the orange coloured, torch shaped object he nearly rammed a car heading in the opposite direction. Fortunately, both motors managed to stop before impact, but the driver of the second vehicle claimed that he had seen nothing of the light which had come so close to causing a serious crash. Both men might be forgiven for believing that the flying orb was a figment, though spectacular, of someone who had not quite 'come to' from an early morning's rising. Curiously, a similar event occurred near Warminster in England, back in 1965 when the area was (as the press named it) the 'UFO Capital' of the Western World. Dozens of UFO sightings were reported. On 10 August 1965 Terry Pell was driving his lorry to Warminster when a 'ball of flaming crimson light ... sped across the sky ... then floated down to his cab in a head-on motion, threatening to smash through the windscreen'. Mr Pell, like Mr Kennedy a decade later, swerved to avoid an impact and ended up over a bank. There were no other witnesses as his wife and daughter, though in the cab with Terry, stayed asleep through the brief but traumatic ordeal. Luckily, however, there were other witnesses to our mysterious Bangour phenomenon that morning. A van driver, also heading west on the A89, towards the town of Broxburn, saw a bright light in the sky. Though stationary, it struck him as too big for a star or planet. The light flashed intermittently on and off, but gradually grew dimmer. Eventually, as nothing else of significance occurred, the driver moved on, but the memory of the strange event remained firmly fixed in his mind.

Around the same time, a young nurse, Anne MacGregor, stepped from her bus and started to walk along the A89 towards Bangour hospital. As she went, Anne heard a distant but distinct hissing noise. Glancing upwards, she caught sight of a bright yellow light that appeared to be descending above the area known as Deans near to a hill called Dechmont Law. This prominence rises on the fringe of the new town of Livingston.

A few minutes later, a cyclist travelling to work at a tyre factory, situated in nearby Newbridge village, stopped to check the traffic flow before making a right turn. As he did so, he spotted a bright yellowish light that appeared to be hovering over the M8 motorway, close to Deer Hill - the local name for Dechmont Law.

Did the object land on Deer Hill? If it did, there are no known witnesses to the touchdown and for the following three hours no more mysterious lights were reported. But then an incident occurred which was to reverberate, and continue to do so, throughout the world wherever UFOs are discussed.

Robert Taylor was well respected as an honest, dedicated forestry worker. A few years off retirement age at 61, Bob was employed by Livingston Development Corporation where he gained an easy familiarity with the woodland areas in the vicinity of the new town. At around 11 a.m. on 9 November Bob, in the company of his dog Lara, a seven year old red setter, was making his way through the covering of fir trees lying on the lower slopes of Dechmont Law. As he approached a clearing in the wood he was shocked to see twelve yards in front of him a large, circular object. According to some accounts it was supported by three metal legs, although Bob himself has not verified this. The object was coloured dark metallic grey and around the circumference Bob noted a distinct though thinnish flange. It did not move, giving Bob more time to note that in parts it seemed transparent, which contrasted sharply with other surfaces which looked like giant sections of emery paper.

Cautiously, Bob approached the mystery visitor. Suddenly, two small spherical devices, similar to those wartime mines with spikes protruding all round, dropped to the ground. It appeared to Bob that they had come from inside the 'craft' and he caught a whiff of a strong, pungent smell which brought on a choking sensation. Over the noise of his dog furiously barking, Bob heard a clear hissing sound (as did nurse Anne MacGregor, recounted earlier). The next thing Bob remembers is coming to, his face pressed hard against the wet ground.

His legs were aching, but through the pain he managed to note that the two spheres and the 'mother' object had disappeared. The barking in his ears confirmed that the faithful Lara had not abandoned him, but Bob could not reassure his dog that he was still alive as he had lost the ability to speak.

In a state of shock, Bob struggled to his feet, was unable to get his lorry started, then staggered the mile back to his home on Broomieknowe Drive in Livingston. It was later suggested that it was during this confused period that Bob ripped his trousers, as he scrambled over a barbed wire fence. The straight, neat line made by the tears, however, would seem to contradict this.

Bob's wife Mary received a terrible shock when she saw the state her husband was in and didn't know what to think when he told her he had been attacked by a spaceship, assuring him 'there's no such thing'. Acting quickly, she phoned the doctor, then Bob's boss, Malcolm Drummond, Head of the Forestry Department, to report the incident. A quick check round Dechmont Law by other forestry workers failed to discover anything out of the ordinary. No sign of an alien craft. Nor of a band of marauding thugs, an explanation which had automatically suggested itself to some who heard of the incident. News travels quickly in this area.

The local police had been alerted and, from their Livingston base, soon arrived at the scene of the 'crime'. Bob joined the officers, headed by Detective Inspector Ian Wark, having insisted on revisiting the spot where he had been attacked. The police and victim noted extensive ladder shaped impressions in the ground just where Bob reckoned the 'craft' had been standing. Indentations revealed the path along which, Bob explained, the spherical objects approached him. Marks in the earth lent support to Bob's belief that he had been dragged towards the larger object before being released.

The police took Bob's account very seriously and a criminal investigation was soon under way. In spite of the extensive publicity, however, and a widespread search, no clue as to the source of Bob's attack was ever unearthed. An 'unsolved' status which confirms the impressions of those who believe that the answer lies outside our worldly realms altogether. The file on Bob's encounter remains open to this day.

The police did confirm in their enquiries that Bob's trousers bore two significant tears which had been made in an upward direction. His legs were cut and bruised in the same area. Someone or something had clearly caught hold of Bob in a grip powerful enough to leave tell-tale marks.

Interest in the incident, now one of the most famous in the annals of ufology, has remained high. Bob Taylor has stood consistently by his account. The character of the man (his boss called him 'sensible and straightforward') has convinced many that an encounter of cosmic significance occurred that day on windswept Dechmont Law.

Understandably, given the closeness of the encounter, those who deny the existence of UFOs have attempted a variety of explanations. Scottish sceptic Steuart Campbell has proposed various possibilities, including ball lightening, a mirage of Venus or Bob's having suffered an epileptic fit. Mr Campbell's solutions have, however, met with little support.

In 1992 Scottish ufologist Ken Higgins and I were instrumental in having a plaque erected to mark the site of this historic incident. It was achieved thanks to the cooperation of Livingston Development Corporation, and the first time that a UFO site has been officially recognised. Sadly, the original plaque was stolen, but plans are being made by SEMR to have a more solid and fitting monument put in its place. Well known sculptor David Annand has produced a design which reflects Mankind's niche in the vast space and unimaginable mysteries of the Universe. It proclaims no solution, but does assume that at this spot a challenge was made to Earth's self-preoccupation.

Mr Taylor's experience also led to Scotland's first UFO song, written by Alan Forrester.

The first verse runs:

> 'It came in over the Pentlands,
> Bob Taylor saw the grey light,
> But no one knows where it came from,
> Riddle of the sky at night.'

Poetic licence, of course, but few could argue that here we have a true 'riddle of the sky'. A riddle which offers the sceptic no easy answer.

Witness accounts of incidents which took place around this time continue to emerge. In October 1992 Mr A Ferguson of Edinburgh reported that while parking his lorry in a lay-by on 8 November 1979 (the time was 8 p.m.) he had noted a strip of brilliant light, shaped like a ruler, heading for Dechmont Law. Another witness, Mrs E Scott, claimed that while she stood at a bus stop gazing towards the Pentland Hills she saw a round silvery object with flashing lights. The first thought that struck her was that it must be a helicopter. In a flash she realised it was nothing of the sort and 'must be a UFO'. She pointed out the mysterious phantom to a lady beside her, who confirmed the strange nature of this visitor. Unfortunately, it has not proved possible to trace this witness. Suddenly, the object shot off at high speed towards Dechmont Law and disappeared. Mrs Scott, understandably given the time lapse, is uncertain of the date of this incident. She is sure, however, that it happened either on the day of Bob's encounter or the previous evening. Whatever the day, it is clear that Dechmont was a hot-bed of strange events around this time.

On the fourteenth anniversary of the encounter SEMR took well known medium Katrina McNab to the site to try and see if any new information could be gleaned. Catriona, through her psychic abilities, confirmed that alien contact did occur that day. She also felt profoundly affected by a burning sensation.

The Dechmont Law sighting was a key incident in the development of Scottish ufology. It put Scotland on the world UFO map, while at the same time inspiring various individuals to enter the neglected area of UFO investigation. Bob Taylor's encounter has never lost its ability to intrigue. Perhaps one day an explanation may emerge.

One thing is clear: the events of 1979, dramatic though they were, mark neither the beginning nor the end of UFOs over the Lothians. As far back as 1958, James Black of Balgreen Road, Edinburgh, saw a long silver-coloured object streaking across the evening sky over Corstorphine Hill, part of which has been straddled since 1913 by the capital's famous zoo. We know, particularly from research in the United States, that UFOs sometimes show a special interest in animal anatomy, even to the extent of dissecting and mutilating their victims. Was this the reason for their visit at that time? We can only speculate. We do know, however, that Mr Black was so impressed by the incident that he painted a picture of the event which was presented to the author by his daughter. It is interesting to note that in 1995 claims of animal mutilation surfaced in the West Lothian area. Investigator David Colman videoed the corpse of a sheep which appeared to have died in a strange fashion. The farmer on whose land the sheep died claimed that it was killed by a fox. The cause of death, however, seemed to be a huge wound around the throat, which looked as if it had been ripped open. This would surely have been beyond the powers of a fox. Might it have been attacked by another animal, perhaps the mysterious 'black cat' which has appeared in various locations in Scotland? In this urban landscape it seems unlikely, but if not then more extreme solutions may have to be considered.

In another early sighting which occurred in 1958, Mrs Lyn Livingston, now a Care Officer, saw 'five or six disc shaped objects, very high up and travelling at speed'. The sighting, in the Sighthill area of the city, lasted only a few seconds before the objects disappeared from view.

From these and other incidents we can conclude, with some certainty, that UFOs have been visiting the Lothians for nearly fifty years.

Yet there appears to be no pattern to these strange visitors which come in differing shapes and can appear almost anywhere. Mysterious balls of fire are frequently seen hovering around the Pentland Hills. Within sight of the lower slopes, for example, where Morton and Black Hill meet, lies an area known as High Camillty. In this isolated spot a glowing ball of light has been observed hovering about twenty feet above the ground, then moving slowly but deliberately towards Camillty Water along the line of the Black Burn. On one occasion, its progress was followed for several minutes by a family from the upstairs window of their detached house. The object was identical to a spherical ball which had trailed a farmer as he walked home at the end of a working day in nearby fields. Here, too, the phenomenon as it moved followed the line of Camillty Water. Is there something peculiarly attractive about the fast-flowing stream with its origins deep in the contours of those mystic Pentland Hills?

These lights appear harmless, but we should recall the UFO encounter on the morning of 9 November 1979, which almost led to an accident. Intention or pure chance? We will not find the answer until we uncover a bit more of this mystery.

Interestingly, these lights are often seen in the vicinity of major roads. On 21 September 1991 a witness travelling to work on the A71 saw a large bright light which kept pace with his car. At the village of Wilkieston about one and a half miles outside Edinburgh the object, which had now changed to a white dome-shape, moved ahead and hovered above the road. Frightened that the strange presence was somehow watching or waiting for him, the witness stopped his car and reversed at speed till he reached a row of shops. The object then accelerated away and disappeared in a south-easterly direction.

The phenomenon continues to make regular appearances. In April 1993 a witness reported a line of bright white lights hovering along the ridge of the Pentland Hills, stretching for several miles. And in November 1994 a motorist on the Edinburgh by-pass saw a shining globe above Caerketton, whose lower slopes border the dual carriageway. One of these mysterious balls has even been caught on video. In November 1995 Brian Curran's home near Polbeth, Bathgate, was 'buzzed by a fireball UFO', according to *The Sun* newspaper. The reporter also claimed that 'the huge blazing craft appeared just yards from them as they cleared up after a party'. Although, in fact, the orange object remained a distance away in the night sky, the film footage was in itself definite enough evidence. The UFO appeared as a bright orange disc and had the characteristics of a three-dimensional object. Its surface was ruffled and although one commentator described it as like a baby's rusk, I would describe it as identical to the famous gong struck at the start of old Rank films. The most intriguing aspects of the mystery object were the two semi-circular gaps, one at the bottom and the second on the lower right, which in the early frames look like monstrous bites out of a round cheese. However, as the video runs, it is as if a mechanism is in operation, and two smooth coated chunks move out of the main body to fill the empty portions. As Brian and his wife Shirley continued watching, the object disappeared, then reappeared, then shot off at an amazing rate and vanished. Air Traffic at Edinburgh Airport claimed there had been no unusual sightings that night. Interestingly, in February 1996 a similar object was filmed over Inverness, and days before the Curran encounter an almost identical UFO was filmed over Norwich in England.

Analysis of Brian Curran's video was undertaken by John Morrison, who following an extensive examination confirmed that an object had definitely been filmed, but was of the opinion that it was in fact arrow shaped rather than oval.

Maureen Buchanan of Musselburgh believes she has seen an orange object identical to the Curran sighting on two separate occasions. The first was at 8 p.m. on 16 November 1992 and again on 22 November 1994 at 10 p.m. The object seen on the second occasion had a 'bite' out of the top left hand corner. Even with video evidence, however, it is unlikely the mystery will be solved.

Inexplicable balls of light travelling in the sky or near the ground may intrigue, but the sceptics will, of course, demand harder evidence. A 48 year old jogger, Ian Atkinson, was making a circuit of Arthur's Seat, that lion shaped hill which dominates the Edinburgh skyline and features so often in descriptions of the city. It was early in the morning of Thursday, 28 October 1992, around ten minutes to seven. 'It was a dark, clear sky', explained Ian, 'no clouds and the stars were visible'. He continued, 'As I was coming round the Radical Road ... just up from the Pollock Halls of Residence, I saw an oval/round object, white and clearly defined'. Ian is a photographer and thus has a keen eye for detail. According to him the object was not glowing, but was sharp edged and definitely solid. Within two seconds it had traversed an incredible distance across the sky. It vanished from sight 'almost as if', Ian added mysteriously, 'someone saw it and the light was switched out'. Time and again key witnesses have reported that eerie feeling that UFOs are aware of the observer's presence.

UFOs, it should be noted, are not necessarily the traditional round or oval form. In fact, they can come in any shape or size. On 8 August 1996, Andrew McMichael of Mortonhall in Edinburgh was woken at two in the morning by a bright fluorescent light bathing his bedroom window. Hovering above the houses on the other side of the street, he could make out an object which he described as similar to a 'K bulb', that is flattened and very bright. He estimated the object's size as 30 feet long and 15 feet high, hovering about 200 feet above the ground. It was distinctly white with cherry red emissions or possibly a light underneath. So bright was the glow made by the UFO that the houses and trees opposite his house seemed to disappear in the intensity of the light. After a few seconds the 'K bulb' tilted and disappeared behind a clump of trees, heading west. The object may have landed in some fields close by. On 6 January 1993 Mrs P Edwards observed a large rectangular shaped object, which drifted slowly across the face of the moon. It was a clear bright night, so the witness and her husband were able to note that the mysterious visitor temporarily obscured at least half of our sister satellite. While they were watching, the rectangle simply faded away before their eyes! To Mrs Edwards the object seemed a good distance away.

Pat Macleod of Portobello got much closer to her UFO. Anyone who has had the good fortune to speak to Pat will emerge with no doubts as to her sincerity and her conviction that what she saw happen did in fact take place. Having interviewed Pat several times and videoed her relating these events, I have no reason to doubt her account. Pat's encounter was considered of such significance that it was included in a SKY TV programme on world-wide ufology.

One morning in October 1992, Pat was driving along Duddingston Park making for the local health centre in Mountcastle Drive to keep an appointment. The time was 9.50 a.m. As she drove, Pat became aware of an extremely bright light in the sky. She noted that it was steady and flashing. Half a mile further on, keeping the light in view, she realised that it was getting bigger and the brightness intensifying. In fact it was drawing much closer to her and as it approached she noted that the central sphere of light had a ring or flange round it. This reminded her, Pat told me, of pictures she had seen of the planet Saturn.

At about twenty to thirty feet from the ground, the object slowed down and appeared to hover. It was large. Very large. The length of an aeroplane wingspan, according to Pat. Around the circumference were placed at regular intervals squares of light, like glowing windows.

Pat had not been checking her watch while this curious event unfolded, but reckons it was now around ten o'clock. She was due at the health centre at that time, and reckons she arrived not too long after.

As she turned off the main road to carry on down a side street to her destination, the object veered east in the opposite direction and slowly descended, seeming to land in an area of open ground called Niddrie Burn: a valley shaped expanse of grass with a stream running (perhaps crawling might be more apt) through the centre. Although it is open land, the ground is, in fact, surrounded by houses and multi-storey flats which have a clear view of the valley. Incredibly, in spite of considerable publicity over the incident, not a single person came forward to testify to having seen the object simultaneously with Pat's sighting. Pat has confirmed to me that there were cars on the road at this time, though heading away from the descending sphere.

How is it possible that something so large and bizarre, an orb so utterly distinctive, was seen by Pat, but passed unnoticed by others. Did Pat misidentify another natural object? Investigation into the possibility that this might be a helicopter proved inconclusive. Although evidence indicated that there had not been any helicopter movement in that area at the time, one cannot be 100% certain. But Pat obviously knows a helicopter when she sees one and is adamant that it does not fit this particular bill! Pat, for example, confirmed that the craft she saw moved silently, which no one can accuse a helicopter of doing. Furthermore, such a noisy machine landing in Niddrie Burn in broad daylight would surely have been spotted and reported. A helicopter as the basis of this incident must be ruled out, particularly if we realise that the object passed within a hundred feet of her car. Pat had every opportunity to make a positive identification. She was so convinced something weird had happened that she called the police to discover whether any other witness had rung in to report the event. Pat then, as now, was determined to have the corroboration to prove the reality of what she saw. She has said that a number of people came into the shop she owned and confirmed that they too had witnessed strange incidents at the time she went through her experience. Not being an investigator into UFO phenomena, Pat did not bother to take their names, an omission she later regretted.

UFO sceptic Steuart Campbell has a completely different explanation for Pat's encounter. He believes that she 'saw a double-merged mirage of Mercury caused by seeing it enlarged via a temperature inversion'. Mr

Campbell points out that Mercury would have been in Pat's line of sight as she drove down Duddingston Park South. He suggests that Pat's description of the object as 'resembling Saturn' is 'a good description of a double-merged mirage of a planet'. Pat's movement in the car may then have created the impression that the object was growing in size and 'landing'. Although this explanation cannot be dismissed, the intense nature of the experience coupled with Pat's detailed observation at close quarters would seem to rule out this scientific explanation.

Interestingly, however, though no other witnesses directly confirmed Pat's sighting, evidence did emerge of curious events that day which back up Pat's account. Jon Jeromsom, who ran a plumbing business in Duddingston Park, was looking out of his showroom window when he saw a bright object descend to about 50 feet. It hovered for several seconds, then vanished. The time? 10 a.m. - at the same moment the object Pat had encountered disappeared from her view. Later that day Mr Jeromsom believes he observed the same light again, poised over a building directly opposite his business at around 4.45 p.m.

The UFO may have returned to the area some months later. On Christmas Day to be exact. Mrs Ann McGuire of Portobello High Street looked out of her bedroom window at 10 p.m. that night and became aware of a black oval shaped object in the night sky. She got a good view of the mysterious visitor as it stood clear of clouds and was sharply defined. She watched it for three minutes, during which time it remained stationary. It made no noise and she was not aware of the object moving away. Later that week when she saw a drawing of Pat's UFO in the *Edinburgh Evening News* she instantly recognised it as the one she had seen.

In June 1995, Ann Beaumont (36) of Niddrie Mains Road had an excellent sighting of an object which resembled Pat Macleod's, but also differed from it in one key aspect. Ann's account in her own words provides an excellent summary of the encounter: 'On Wednesday 7 June 1995 I awoke in the early hours of the morning, 2.15 a.m. according to my bedside clock. For some reason I was drawn to my bedroom window, where I drew back the curtains and looked out onto the deserted street below. From my third floor, I looked out over the east side of Edinburgh and could see it was a dry clear night with little or no breeze. Initially, facing due south, my attention was caught by a slow moving, very low, flying object approaching from the east. It was heading in my direction with a trajectory that followed my plane of view. The closer it came, the more I realised something wasn't quite right. It was flying far too low and didn't have any wings. In other words, it wasn't an aeroplane. Even at this close range the craft did not make a sound. Throughout my observation, which lasted from 2.15 to 2.30 a.m. (again, confirmed by my bedroom clock) the craft neither increased nor decreased its altitude or velocity. Unfortunately, I couldn't make out its colour due to the intensity of its lights'. Ann meant that its overall hue could not be judged, but bright red and white lights were visible around the circumference of the UFO. The picture of the object that she drew shows an 'upturned cup' shape with a distinct flange. Porthole-like openings were arranged at regular intervals across the upper area. George Niedzwiedz, an investigator with the British Unidentified Flying Object Research Association (BUFORA) confirms that no definite solution has been arrived at as yet.

My inquiries into the Macleod sighting uncovered a very curious incident which, although it did not link directly into Pat's encounter, had taken place in a house overlooking Niddrie Burn a few days before. The witness woke up in the early hours of the morning, she isn't sure why, and caught sight of a brilliant white light clearly visible through her bedroom window. She tried to draw her husband's attention to the phenomenon, but he stayed resolutely asleep. Curious and slightly apprehensive, she got out of bed and went to the window to take a closer look. She noticed that the light seemed to be coming towards the window. Her attention was drawn to a tree at the foot of her garden. Poised on one of the thicker branches stood a thing which she described as 'a giant bird' the size of a man or possibly a human-like figure with wings. Was this the only Scottish sighting of Mothman, the mysterious creature which has been encountered across the Atlantic in various parts of the United States? Badly frightened by what she had seen, she tried again to wake up her partner who would not move and gave the impression of being in a trance. She climbed into bed, and as she did so, a light came into the room and moved along the wall till it had travelled all the way round back to its starting point. The witness remained in a highly nervous state till, as dawn broke, she at last fell asleep.

Could the mysterious object glimpsed by Jon Jeromsom be the same one observed by Pat Macleod? Or, even more incredible, the same one that was witnessed several miles away the year before? There are definite similarities. A couple from the village of Ladywell near Livingston in West Lothian were looking from their back room window when they spotted a bright light in the sky. It was 10.30 p.m. on a clear August night in 1991. They could be sure of the time as ITN's regular news programme had just gone off the air. Both husband and wife were familiar with plane lights as the flight path to nearby Turnhouse Airport, servicing Edinburgh, passes close to the house. It was precisely because this sighting didn't fit into the pattern of approaching aircraft that it first attracted their attention. Its appearance struck them both as being completely out of the ordinary. They were so intrigued by the spectacle and the fact that the light made no attempt to move but simply hovered, that Mr John Grant took out his binoculars to take a closer look.

What he saw fascinated him. He could make out a pyramid shaped object with a series of lights clustered at each corner. Both he and his wife were now certain that there was a solid mysterious presence hovering over the electricity pylons in the field outside their village. Drawing some strange sustenance, perhaps? As they watched the object for a full twenty minutes through field glasses, there can be no doubt that they witnessed an incident that was outside the normal. A quick phone call to Turnhouse Air Traffic Control produced the startling response that nothing was showing up on radar! The visitor disappeared as suddenly and unexpectedly as it had arrived.

The appearance of the object capped a twenty four hour period of strange incidents for the family. The night before, as they lay in bed, a brilliant beam of light unexpectedly illuminated their bedroom. It shone with such intensity that it turned night into day. Both Pat and John leapt from their bed in an attempt to discover the source of the strange illumination. The light, however, having swept the four walls, had vanished and taken with it the secret of its origins. Neither husband nor wife could discover any obvious cause for this unique phenomenon.

An investigation by Ken Higgins and me soon after came to the same conclusion - there was no obvious explanation for the event. The position of the bedroom windows and doors made it highly unlikely that the incident could have been caused by something as mundane as passing car lights. They would have had to shine through a landing window before penetrating the doorway and the angle involved ruled out this as a possibility. Nor was there an object from which a light may have been reflected into the room. Again, the direction and intensity of the illumination meant that such a solution could not be seriously entertained. Furthermore, the beam entered *horizontally* and thus an overhead source, such as a helicopter, had to be eliminated. It is noteworthy that the family reported no noise evident at the time of the experience.

The incident, therefore, must enter the 'unexplained' category, despite having additional witnesses. Neighbours of the Grants who live directly opposite experienced the same beam of light travelling through their home. They, similarly, could detect no obvious source for this ray. But is there a connection between this event and the pyramid shape seen hovering in the area? No immediate link springs to mind. Yet it is strange that two such curious incidents should happen within hours of each other involving the same family. Publicity about the incidents covered by journalist David Cowan, then of the *Lothian Courier*, brought an intriguing response. A nurse rang in to say that she and a companion had seen in the same area a pulsating beam of light shining from a dark object. The timing of the sighting at 10.35 p.m. coincided with that of Pat and John Grant.

The previous night (4 August) a family walking their dog in the Ladywell area observed an orange coloured light partly hidden by a tree. When they approached it, the light disappeared. At the time of writing no answer to this bizarre miscellany of events is forthcoming. Interestingly, however, the area was noted for the appearance of a ghost. One similarity between apparitions and UFOs is that a ghost may appear in a room and not everyone will see it. This is also the case with UFOs. A UFO may appear in broad daylight, but only one person may report the encounter even though to the witness the object is so clear that they are convinced many people would have seen it. I have no answer, at present, to the conundrum.

Although it is speculation, there may be a connection between the Ladywell triangle and a UFO sighted over the Forth Railway Bridge. This mysterious incident took place on 7 October 1990, at approximately 9.15 p.m. Lynn and Alex Livingston were watching a firework display to mark the centenary of the opening of the railway link over the Forth. It was a clear windless night. High in the sky Lynn suddenly noticed a circular shaped object, formed by a battery of red, white and blue lights. It appeared to twinkle and rotate, changing from a circle to a shallow cone shape. The object remained in view for a full fifteen minutes, almost as if wishing to be observed, growing dimmer as either the strength of the lights faded or it drifted northwards over the Fife coast. The *Sunday Mail* headlined the incident 'UFO Joins in Forth Bridge Celebrations'. It should be remembered, however, that many key military installations lie on the borders of the Forth Estuary.

Could the Forth Bridge visitation have had any connection with another mysterious object that has been plaguing the skies over the Lothians? On 16 August 1992 a Bathgate couple, Mr and Mrs Tait, witnessed a strange incident, one which had them rushing to their telephone. At 10.15 p.m. exactly they saw an intense green light travelling from east to west on a downward trajectory and appearing to impact with the earth about half a mile from their house. Convinced that they had been unwitting observers of a plane crash, they rang Turnhouse Airport to report the incident. To their relief and surprise, they discovered that no aircraft were in the area at the time. Whatever they had seen, it was clearly not an aeroplane.

A few days later, following a telephone call, I met and spoke with the couple. Both hold down responsible jobs (one is a teacher) and had nothing to gain from reporting the incident. In between hearing of this event and visiting Mr and Mrs Tait, I heard from Nicholas Reid, then a twenty-two year old law graduate living in Broxburn. He confirmed seeing a 'stream of green light which was travelling 45 degrees towards the earth'. Nicholas awaited the inevitable impact and from his window scanned 'nearby fields for any evidence of fire'. To his surprise, however, he could detect no evidence of a crash.

With Nicholas's account backing up the Taits' description, I was convinced that something strange had occurred that night. This emerged even more strongly when Ken Higgins, checking back through his files, reported that an almost identical event had occurred at a bing in nearby Boghall in the 1980s. Several witnesses had observed a green light hit the ground and burst into flames. Mr Tait was certain that he knew roughly where his UFO had come down. I was taken to the spot, called Riddochhill, where it seemed the impact crater might be found. The area had once been an important coal mining location, but had long been disused and eventually in-filled with a view to long term development. At one end a black scurry revealed where the old mine workings began. Marks scarred the surface of one slope, produced perhaps by an object hitting the ground at speed. I was so excited by this evidence that I took several pictures for SEMR's photographic library. Apart from these marks, however, there was little else to be seen, in spite of a search which covered a substantial part of the infill.

The reason for this emerged over the following weeks. It is a reminder that no serious investigator should get too easily carried away! The initial incident was covered by reporter Ian Kyle of *The Edinburgh Evening News*. As a result, new witnesses called in and it became obvious that the object had not come down near Bathgate, but travelled several miles further west. A family living in the village of Blackburn reported that they had seen the object descend from the sky and land to the rear of their house. Again, for fear of ridicule in a small community, the family did not wish to be named. When I visited the family, however, the evidence that came from the grandmother and grandson was very firm. An intense green ball had come from the sky and seemed to hit the earth behind a line of trees in open farmland, a few hundred yards from their comfortably furnished terraced house.

An investigation of this undulating countryside was carried out by

Ken Higgins and myself, assisted by dowser Mary Land and Ian Shanes, a psychic medium from Glasgow. Although this survey turned up many points of interest, it failed to discover any sign of an impact crater or landing marks. Whatever the object was, or is, it seemed to have disappeared as mysteriously as it arrived. One fact did emerge, however, through a chance conversation with a local farmer. Ten years previously, a strange *yellow* object had travelled over the same farmland visited by our green light phenomenon. It seemed as if the Cosmic Joker had been at work once more.

Interest in the green light continued unabated, and from all over the Lothians witnesses came forward to testify to having seen this strange object. Mrs Adriane Goldie, a Mid Calder housewife, reported seeing green lights on 15 October 1992 'darting about in a zig-zag pattern as if they were playing'. Some cases, it emerged, stretched back several years. As long ago as 1981 Marion Findlay from Edinburgh wrote to *The Daily Record*, describing a bright green light travelling across the sky, moving 'too fast to be a plane'. Like the Bathgate couple, however, Mrs Findlay's husband 'thought it might be a plane crashing'.

Returning to more recent times, William Mackay from Glasgow, who was carrying out lighting tests on the roof of St Cuthbert's Church in Edinburgh, on 27 October 1992 saw 'a very luminous green light' moving at speed at around 7.10 p.m. It travelled from 'east to west from Edinburgh Castle to Usher Hall, where it disappeared into a cloud'. Mr Mackay added that the object 'was brightly coloured and appeared to leave a disappearing green vapour trail'.

In passing, it is interesting to note that the Jewish astronomer Flegetanis identified the Holy Grail as a green stone fallen from the skies. Students of Earth Mysteries will note the existence in the Lothians of Rosslyn Chapel and its association with legends of the Grail and hidden arcane knowledge. Of course, if you are convinced that UFOs are nuts-and-bolts extraterrestrial spacecraft, you will view the connection as pure coincidence.

One scientific explanation put forward for the numerous green light sightings is that they are meteors. However, the quantity of the objects seen and size and intensity of the light rules this theory out in the majority of cases, though certainly not all. In specific cases such as the 16 August 1992 incident where a meteorite trajectory can be pinpointed, the timing does not match that of the event noted by witnesses. Whatever was seen that night, it was not that particular (and by all accounts spectacular) meteor entry. In this case it is the sceptics who need to check their facts!

The difficulty in arriving at a solution to the green light phenomenon is shown by contradictory testimony the author received from witnesses who observed the object 'landing' near the village of Blackburn. On 20 October 1992 a senior policeman who saw the event wrote to me. He had been measuring a window for curtains when around 10 p.m. he 'became aware of a cluster of bright white and green lights in the sky immediately to the north-east of the town'. He concedes that 'the light formation did look rather unusual' but believes that 'this may have been due to the angle ... I was viewing it (from)'. The light cluster then split in two, one side 'dipping sharply at an angle of approximately forty-five degrees, before levelling off and continuing northwards at a reasonably fast speed'. Meanwhile, the 'other half of the light cluster moved off in the opposite direction at a slow speed, but without appearing to change altitude'. Not unreasonably, this observer, viewing from Blackburn, came to the conclusion he had been watching 'two domestic or military aircraft which suddenly changed direction or flight path'.

I put this explanation to the other Blackburn witnesses. They were quite definite that the series of events described by the policeman did not fit what they had seen. They had definitely observed a single bright object which had come down in the vicinity of their village. Could there have been two separate green lights that night? It appears unlikely given the close timing. Yet all the witnesses are adamant about their interpretation of what they saw. The opposing testimony makes it difficult to draw firm conclusions. It has been argued that UFOs which appear as bright lights can be explained as emanating from the earth itself. Spheres of energy produced by rock under pressure. The term 'earthlight' was coined by leading earth mysteries researcher Paul Devereux in his 1982 book of the same name. Leading British ufologist Jenny Randles applied this theory to specific incidents in her book *The Pennine UFO Mystery* (1983). It is also argued that electromagnetic disturbance affects individual perception and so leads to reports of UFOs. It cannot be denied that rock stress occurs in the West Lothian area. It is well known for its fault lines and occasional earth tremors. So the idea of earth lights rather than extraterrestrial lights has to be taken seriously (providing the initial proposition is accepted, which it is not by all scientists). On the other hand, the distance covered by the green light and manoeuvres associated with it seem to work against so 'down-to-earth' an explanation. It is interesting to note that the green light phenomenon occurs throughout the British Isles and that it is, particularly in Scotland, regarded as an omen forewarning of misfortune. It would, indeed, be apt if these strange balls turned out in reality to be the warning signs of a forthcoming earthquake.

If John is to be believed, however, the earthquake when it arrives will be psychological rather than physical. How will we cope with the realisation that extraterrestrials not only exist, but are amongst us even as we read this text? John is nothing if not totally honest. He knows he could make his story easier to believe by withholding details, but is brave enough to give the whole picture, not simply selected titbits.

John is a 45 year old ex-engineer who lives beside the Forth and Clyde Canal in a small West Lothian town. He experienced psychic phenomena as a child, but strange incidents only started again in 1991. John has kept a diary of the odd events which have occurred and it is an extensive list. It would not be possible to describe every encounter, but a general picture of the evidence will, I believe, show just what a mysterious world we live in. To those who would question 'Why should it happen in West Lothian?', the answer surely is 'Why not?'

John is a tall, thin, thoughtful man who has considered carefully the strange incidents which have centred on him and his semi-detached cottage. On 23 December 1994 he was sitting watching television when suddenly the picture went haywire. Crazy patterns formed across the screen before it blanked off. In the kitchen, the emergency lighting, running on batteries, went dead. The next thing John remembers is being in a room with no windows. Looking over him was one 'human looking alien'. John wasn't the only 'visitor'. Sitting on a bench were four young men staring blankly as if they couldn't believe what they were seeing. The entity turned to John and warned him, 'Don't go and investigate', then walked through a door into what appeared to be a corridor. It struck John forcibly then that *he may not have been in a ship, but in a building*. An awesome possibility. John was tempted, strongly tempted, to follow the being into the corridor and open a door, one of several he could see at regular intervals breaking the smooth contours of the craft's walls. However a silent voice seemed to warn him that if he did he would see something that might not be particularly pleasant. Perhaps some form of alien entity. At this point John 'woke up' to find himself back in bed with the room bathed in red light.

From another experience John can give a good description of the interior of an alien craft. It was between 15 to 20 feet in diameter and, on this occasion, he found himself standing on a partly raised balcony on the outside edge, which was about a metre wide. The floor of the UFO was formed by shiny metal slats like polished aluminium. They appeared disc shaped, perhaps even forming a pattern. The walls had been welded from the same material, although here it took the form of panels.

In the middle of the room stood a couch shaped object, more like one found in an operating theatre than in the average home. John could remember fine details, even down to the black cushion lying on the 'table'. The austere atmosphere of the room was broken by a single window, gently curved, which ran from floor to ceiling. Perhaps sensing his curiosity, two creatures, which inexplicably he could not see but could feel, lifted him up to the window and he could look out at the panorama of the universe stretching before him.

When John 'came to' in his bedroom, again around 4 a.m., he noticed puncture marks in his neck. Small red ones, which felt itchy and sore as if a cluster of hypodermic needles had been forced into his skin.

John's experience would swallow up a chapter on its own. Many incidents lie outside the scope of this book because they involve powerful spiritual imagery. The view that aliens and traditional religious figures such as angels are linked in some strange way has gained currency in recent years. Who can say that within the cross-currents of religion may not be hidden the rock of truth to solve the UFO mystery?

One encouraging aspect is that John feels that the aliens have attempted to heal him. He suffers from a number of maladies, including arthritis. After a visit from the entities John, who had difficulty walking any distance, found that he could walk a mile with ease. Maybe these are friends rather than something to be feared. Indeed, some argue that our government and aliens are already enjoying an '*entente cordiale*'.

In spite of their denials, it is clear that the Ministry of Defence and the armed forces are very much interested in UFO encounters. In April 1995 a commercial airline pilot, Ray, brought his cargo into Edinburgh Airport from the East Midlands. It was a regular run and he had landed well on time, the hands on the dial pointing to one o'clock. It had been a clear night and the flight had been trouble free. As Ray taxied off the runway away from the passenger terminal, he noticed a lot of excitement among the British Airways security staff. He learned that Air Traffic Control had caught an unidentified object on radar hovering near the airport. There had been a visual sighting confirming the presence of the UFO. As air traffic monitored its passage, one cargo plane from Gill Aviation, based in Newcastle, approached on a landing course. Edinburgh asked the pilot to take a look at the strange object but he was unable to confirm the report. On the surface, therefore, there seems to have been several well qualified witnesses to an unidentified flying object.

Or were there? A week later, Ray was back in Edinburgh and asked Air Traffic if they had reached any conclusion about the mysterious visitor. He was met by a blank wall. The tower denied all knowledge, claiming they didn't know what he was talking about. Mystified, Ray mentioned it to colleagues. A fresh and even stranger tale emerged. He was told that RAF Kinloss had scrambled three Tornado aircraft to investigate objects which, it seemed, appeared as a bright white light at an altitude of two to three thousand feet. As the fighters approached, they shot straight up and disappeared. My own attempt to confirm this incident met with a firm, but extremely speedy, denial from the Ministry of Defence. Gill Aviation failed to respond to my requests for information, all in all confirming my suspicion that whether or not it was a visitor from another planet, something strange was seen over Edinburgh that day.

Although over the last decade West Lothian can claim pride of place as the area which has experienced a UFO wave, this has not always been the case. In the 1950s the county town of Haddington was the UFO hot spot of Scotland. The Reverend Joseph Ritchie, for example, saw a round, silver coloured object which disappeared in the direction of the Lammermuir Hills. In November of the same year fourteen 'tattie howkers' witnessed a strange flying object which appeared from the direction of the North Sea. These and other cases were investigated by local expert John Sparks, founder of the Scottish UFO Research Society which flourished at the end of that decade. Mr Sparks helped to arrange the visit of contactee George Adamski to Edinburgh in 1958, when he addressed a packed meeting at Central Hall, Tollcross.

However, events in recent years have propelled East Lothian back into the news. Strange orange balls of light were seen travelling over both land and sea. One of the first incidents was reported by Mrs Coutts of Dunbar. On Thursday 11 January 1995 she was travelling from Dunbar to Edinburgh. At 11.05 a.m. her car had reached the Beltonford roundabout, where the main A1 trunk road meets the A1087. As she glanced towards the Firth of Forth she caught sight of an orange circular ball travelling in a straight line at about tree top height. Mrs Coutts, however, also stated that its altitude could be equated to a low flying aeroplane, so that it would probably be correct to assume that the object was a few hundred feet from the ground rather than thirty or forty. She was sure, however, that the UFO was not a plane as she was familiar with their movements. Furthermore, it was a clear day with a bright January sun. Mrs Coutts found it difficult to give a more detailed description of the object she saw, but did say it reminded her of something glowing hot. So convinced was she that she had seen something odd that she was certain that others must also have seen it. She knew it had travelled towards Dunbar golf course and felt that anyone out playing that day would have been bound to have seen it. She suggested I contact the local paper, *The East Lothian Courier*, in case other witnesses had called in.

My resulting appeal brought in several witnesses, including a possible explanation. Mrs M McNeill informed me that there were several orange balls attached to cables close to where the 11 January sighting occurred and that this might explain the incident. It is, however, clear that there had been a variety of objects seen around the same period. What was intriguing was that the reports, although differing in a variety of details, brought together similar aspects. Had the same object been seen for several years over the East Lothian area?

Monica Cameron wrote to me describing an 'orange star' and 'three small flashing lights moving in the sky'. At first she assumed it was an aeroplane, but then noticed that one of the lights was moving faster than the other two. As the faster moving light caught up with the slower one, 'the slower light just disappeared'. The light then hovered in the air for a few seconds, before heading back in the direction from which it had come.

Two years previously John Bridges, then a twenty year old farmer, had also witnessed a pulsating light. This encounter occurred on 29 October 1992 as he drove between Haddington and Pencaitland. Beside a wood to his left, Mr Bridges caught sight of a brown coloured object which he described as 'the size of two cars on top of each other'. The UFO was only 400 yards away from him at the time and about 100 feet off the ground. So although it was 11 o'clock at night, the sky was clear and he got a good look at it. He could be sure of what he had seen because at the base of the UFO was a big light which lit up both the object and the surrounding area.

The golden light phenomenon had also appeared on Christmas Day when Mrs Aitken from Musselburgh rang UFO investigator Ken Higgins to inform him that zig-zags of gold were traversing the sky to the east of Musselburgh. Then in November 1995 Thomas McGreig and his wife saw two red lights hovering over the Firth of Forth. However, it remains a mystery as to why orange and gold objects and pulsating lights should be seen so frequently in the area.

One of the strangest UFO sightings in recent years stems from the heart of Scotland's agricultural area in East Lothian. Maureen Clark, a 49 year old housewife from Edinburgh, was travelling on Saturday 31 October

1992 (Halloween!) through the county. As she passed south of Haddington her husband, who was driving their car, noticed a bright light which he judged to be over a nearby hill, just below the cloud line. It was 3.45 p.m. on a cold though dry and windless afternoon. Mrs Clark describes the object as 'a bright light tinged with yellow, not a white light like a spotlight, more mellow'. The light appeared to be circular, 'but flattened on top with a dark mark'.

They managed to keep the light under observation as their journey pulled them closer to the source, The object, meanwhile, remained stationary until their car drew alongside the hill. Then, according to Maureen, it suddenly shot 'very quickly upwards into the clouds'. Up to that point the sky had seemed smothered in grey cloud. But now a break appeared at the exact spot into which the light had disappeared! Through the gap the couple could make out a thick, white, vertical column of a cloud-like substance, resembling a vapour trail. However, it was much denser, wider and straighter edged, starting at cloud level and pointing heavenwards. The mystified pair searched the sky for the cause of the phenomenon, but could see no obvious explanation. Certainly, there was no sign of the strange object initially observed, which now seemed to have disappeared. In Scottish UFO sightings we can find no exact parallel to this mysterious incident.

Curiously, however, Malcolm Archibald of Gorebridge may have seen something similar in reverse. A column of bright lights 'apparently connected, descending at great speed'. As is frequently the case they, or it, 'vanished very suddenly' in the 'vicinity of the Pentland Hills'.

Are we dealing here with objects from beyond the stars, or another dimension? Or can we locate the source in the bowels of the earth? Do flying balls of light prove the existence of 'earthlights' rather than extraterrestrials? Consider the following two cases and make up your own mind.

At two o'clock on the morning of 4 December 1995, Mrs Allan of Cockenzie was driving along North Grange Avenue near the town of Prestonpans. Glancing in her rear view mirror, she caught an unexpected sight. Travelling towards her at a furious rate was a bright ball of glowing green light. She was struck by its huge size, as large as a car, and its direct line of movement, as if locked onto an invisible source. Before she had time to be frightened, it soared over her head at house roof height and shot up into the night sky. In its wake it left a trail of red light. This incident made such an impact on Mrs Allan that she contacted Edinburgh Airport which (UFO investigators will be interested to learn) asked her to complete a questionnaire on her encounter. Paul Devereux, renowned earth mysteries investigator and for many years editor of *The Ley Hunter*, was convinced that this incident was indeed an example of an earthlight. I have to agree that the evidence for this is strong. In pursuing my enquiries, I contacted the British Geological Survey in Edinburgh. Peter Morrison of the Global Seismology Research Group wrote to me on 14 June 1995. 'We have no explanation for the phenomenon observed by the lady near Prestonpans on 4 December last. Earthlights have been reported as a phenomenon accompanying very large earthquakes and that can be discounted in this case! Earthlights, however, have also been reported where earthquakes are absent, so I am not wholly convinced by this, although the existence of such lights seems a recognised fact'.

With the Allan sighting there was no evidence of intelligent life controlling the object. The same is not true of the object seen by Mr and Mrs Buckley of Musselburgh. In the early hours of a cold and frosty winter morning in 1981 (the month was either November or December) they were walking along a pavement close to their house when they spotted an object which appeared like a brilliant white tennis ball. It was hovering beside a lamppost and at first glance the couple took it for a lamplight. Then, however, it started to move. As it did so, they realised that there were, in fact, two balls close together. As the objects moved closer Mr and Mrs Buckley were struck by the intense whiteness of the two balls, 'a fierce white colour', Mrs Buckley vigorously described it. They looked like 'metal, boiling hot'. When first seen the objects were about twenty feet off the ground, but they descended to within an inch or so off the pavement, then moved in front of the Buckleys as they walked along the street. What makes the incident even more intriguing was that the couple felt that the balls seemed 'to have a mind of their own' and 'it was as if the balls were playing a game with us'. Furthermore one ball 'seemed more dominant than the other'. Strange though this encounter may be, it does correspond to incidents reported from other parts of the world and documented in Paul Devereux's book *Earthlights*.

In a sense we have come full circle. Bright lights and the Pentland Hills seem to go together. In *Mysteries of the Scottish Landscape*, I argued that the Lothian area was a place of special and mysterious significance. The focus for that was the Pentland Hills. I also pointed out that in December (the period of the Winter equinox) the silhouette of the hills can give the appearance of a great goddess figure. There is no argument that the whole of the Lothians are riddled with ancient sites of mystic significance. Cairnpapple, near Bathgate, with its neolithic temple, is reckoned to be one of the most important examples of its kind in Europe. Arthur's Seat boasts a plethora of prehistoric settlements. Did the ancients of times past recognise that this area possessed some strange significance? Have UFOs been visiting these parts for perhaps thousands of years? It is a question to which we may never have the answer, although time may well provide an explanation to the UFO enigma.

TWO

A STRANGE VISITATION

The Perthshire region of Scotland, better known for its tourist haunts, has been for many years host to a series of bizarre UFO incidents. The focus of this activity has been the attractive village of Blairgowrie situated on the banks of the River Ericht. During the summer months, visitors arrive from all parts of Britain to explore its scenic hillsides, unaware of the strange events that have periodically shattered the quiet harmony of the countryside and the lives of the local people.

Take Sid Freeman. Sid is a talented craftsman and artist who built up a considerable reputation in restoring antique furniture. It's a down-to-earth occupation, and one that could hardly prepare him for the strange encounter that was to significantly change his family's entire life.

April 25 1984 dawned over the bungalow at Riverside Road, Blairgowrie, and passed peacefully till tea-time. At 5.30 p.m. Mrs Gwen Freeman, Sid's mother, occupied the sun lounger in the back garden, weaving a tapestry. Sid, meanwhile, was at the front, working diligently to clear a flowerbed of weeds. Suddenly, Gwen noticed the family dog cowering and stared in amazement as it ran into the kitchen, its tail tucked between its legs.

Seconds later her attention was caught by a strange cloud (as she described it) of light which enveloped and then, for a split second, actually blinded her. A sensation of warmth crept over her body, focusing on the abdomen. Directly in front, less than five feet from the lounger, a forsythia bush sprang into life, shimmering with sparkly lights. Pulling herself to her feet, Mrs Freeman stood enraptured by this beautiful sight.

Her attention was caught next by a light beam which flowed upwards from the bush, travelled between two fir trees and passed over the roof of the garden shed. Gwen followed the beam skywards where it led to a silvery shape, hovering over her house. Stepping to the side she was able to catch a fuller view of the object, realising as she did so that she was confronting a truly awesome phenomenon. It looked like a 'spaceship' of bizarre design. Gwen later described the object as a large, bulbous shaped thing with a long tail. Beneath the tail section, a light illuminated five V shaped ports. As she observed this, the front of the 'spaceship' lit up and she noticed that a lip or flange surrounded the circular area. Suddenly the port lights were extinguished and the whole length of the object began to rock from front to back.

The shock of witnessing this hovering phantom had driven all other thoughts from Gwen's mind, but, as if a block had shifted from her brain, she instinctively shouted to Sid, 'You'll never guess what I'm looking at! Come quickly before it goes'.

Anxious to find out what had caused so much excitement, Sid immediately left the weeds in peace and hurried to the fence that separated the front and back gardens. To his regret, he paused for a split second before following Gwen's finger, pointing skywards. The object was rapidly diminishing in size and intensity. A bright flash followed, and the UFO was gone.

At this point Gwen's husband, Sid senior, arrived on the scene. Unfortunately, he had not witnessed the encounter. He had been gardening directly in front of the bungalow out of sight of both Gwen and the hovering object. From where he knelt the 'spaceship' was hidden from view by a cluster of overhanging trees. Sid, however, was intrigued by the incident and together the family attempted to estimate the size of the object Gwen and her son had seen. They judged it to be around one hundred and fifty feet in length, floating about eighty feet above the ground. They all agreed that in shape it reminded them exactly of a yale key!

Back indoors the family called in the local police. Two officers quickly arrived. One remarked to his colleague, perhaps not intending Sid to hear, that the 'yale key' sounded just like an object that had already been reported over Blairgowrie. The officers then moved outside and thoroughly searched the garden, taking soil samples from the area where Mrs Freeman had been sitting, and collecting leaves from the forsythia bush. After about two hours, and many questions later, the policemen left, telling the family that they would keep them informed of the outcome of the investigation. In fact, from that day to this the Freemans have not heard one more word from the police. Why, it may be asked, the secrecy? Attempts in the early 1990s by UFO investigator Ken Higgins to locate police reports met with a blank wall. No-one at the police station claimed to remember the incident and informed Ken that any documents relating to it would have been transferred and probably destroyed.

The family's strange encounter was the start and not the end of a period of strange events. One morning Sid and Gwen heard an unusual rumbling above the house. The noise grew louder and closer until it reached deafening heights and the whole bungalow seemed to vibrate. Looking from the back door, they were shocked to see a large military helicopter hovering some forty feet above the house. Underneath the 'chopper' were slung two box-like devices, one black and the other orange. They were hanging so close to the roof that Gwen could see a small red light on top of one of the boxes. It seemed that the crew were filming the area around the Freeman home. From the way the helicopter was moving they gained the impression that it was testing the air. In the light of the family's encounter, if it was a coincidence, it seemed a remarkable one indeed.

Sid phoned the nearest RAF station, Leuchars, to find out just what was going on. After some initial difficulty, he was informed that the helicopter was simply 'on manoeuvres', and that there was nothing for the family to worry about. Two days later, however, they were startled by the reappearance of the helicopter and were struck by the fact that it repeated the earlier tests. Manoeuvres again?! Significantly, the RAF had not chosen Blairgowrie previously to carry out exercises, nor have they found it a suitable spot since.

When I visited Sid in the summer of 1991, the events of those days were very clear in his mind. As I listened in quiet fascination, it seemed impossible that Sid could surprise me with any further revelations. I was wrong, however. For the first time, Sid told me of an event the very morning of Gwen Freeman's sighting which, because of its strange nature, convinced me that it could not be invented.

Some time before midday on April 25, Mrs Freeman called her son to the window. Both watched in silent wonder as a group of strangely dressed men walked quietly up the deserted street. The sight was remarkable: some twelve men, all dressed in black Yiddish attire, wearing hats of the same colour and several with pigtails stretching down their backs.

An unusual scene for a Blairgowrie resident to witness! Sid's curiosity, however, turned to anxiety when the group of strangers walked up the path of a neighbour's house, then disappeared inside without even bothering to ring the doorbell. Gwen was struck by one other odd fact. The twelve had kept moving in deliberate single file, a regular space between each one, from the moment they had caught her attention to the time they entered the next door bungalow. One stranger fact: not one word was uttered by the men in black during all that time.

Gwen and Sid now felt themselves in a quandary. They had no wish to be nosey, but as good friends of the woman next door they were concerned for her safety. Just as they had made up their minds to go and investigate, the same twelve came out of the front door, still in single file, and walked back the way they had come. Sid noticed that once again not one of these mysterious figures exchanged so much as a word with his colleague. Convinced that something odd had taken place, Sid and Gwen decided to make sure that nothing had happened to harm their friend.

They rang the doorbell, then waited anxiously. The door was soon opened by their friend, who seeing their worried faces asked what the matter was! Taken aback, Sid explained why he and Gwen had called round, describing the strange figures they had seen on her garden path. Visibly stunned for a second or two, a smile then creased her lips, as if to say, 'Is this April Fool's Day?' It was clear as far as she was concerned that no one, and certainly not mysterious men in black, had entered her house either that or any other day. Grasping this, the Freemans were in turn staggered, embarrassed and worried. Muttering apologies, Sid and Gwen hurried home.

Of course, accounts of mysterious 'men in black' or MIBs will be familiar to anyone who has the slightest knowledge of the subject of UFOs. In the book *Fact or Fantasy*, Hilary Evans discussed several such cases. Typical is that of September 1976 involving Dr Herbert Hopkins of Maine, USA, who was acting as a consultant in an alleged UFO case. He was telephoned by a man claiming to be a UFO investigator, who shortly afterwards arrived at his door dressed in a black scarf, black tie and black shoes, wearing a hat of identical colour. The visitor behaved in such a strange way that Hopkins 'was very much shaken' by the incident. The implication of this MIB encounter was that the mysterious caller was not of this world. Although in this case no car was in evidence, a black coloured cadillac has traditionally been linked to this type of incident. The Freeman case has similarities to Dr Hopkins' tale, that is a UFO event associated with the appearance of odd individuals in black apparel, but it seems clear that in Blairgowrie we have a different type of encounter. MIBs are usually described as relatively contemporary in dress and seeking out information from the witnesses themselves. What the Freemans saw comes across as being more of a religious or psychic experience. Or even a combination of the two. It does often seem to be the case that aspects of the UFO enigma take on (despite our best efforts to ignore them) spiritual aspects. Furthermore, the men in black were seen before the UFO incident rather than after it. Had they in some strange way made a mistake about the time of the UFO sighting? Were they supposed to link up with the hovering UFO? Admittedly, it is all speculation, but it is even harder to believe that the timing of these two incidents was the product of pure chance.

Over the next week or so the family did their best to push that strange incident to the back of their minds. They wanted to forget it. But fate, it seemed, had determined otherwise.

One evening the doorbell rang. Mrs Freeman turned down the volume on the television and went to answer the door. On the porch she discovered two strangers, a man and woman dressed in old-fashioned, 1920s style clothing. His was a dark pin-striped suit, reminiscent of the gangster era, with a hat to match. She hid inside a long, flowing coat, and Gwen was struck by her headdress which would have done service as a bowl of fruit! Yet at the time, Gwen did not find the two strangers the slightest bit funny. A dark air hung about them.

The couple spoke to her in English, but sounded as if they had each swallowed a bible. They told Gwen that 'she must not speak more of what she had seen otherwise a great evil would befall her'. Other threats followed in quick succession. Alarmed by what was being said, Sid and his father hurried to the door and ordered the unwanted visitors to leave. They swung round to face each other and, without expression or exchanging words, walked down the path, turned and headed towards the village. They never returned and were not reported elsewhere in Blairgowrie on that or any other day. Was it a message devised by the authorities to keep them quiet? Or simply a pair of cranks? Sid asked himself. The alternatives seemed too bizarre to contemplate.

Sid, of course, was not a UFO buff and so was not familiar with similar incidents. The daughter-in-law of Dr Hopkins (whose encounter was mentioned earlier) was rung by a couple who asked to meet them. When they arrived, the first thing she noticed was their strangely *old-fashioned clothes*. Their conversation and manner of speech did not seem normal - and when they left, they both walked in a *perfectly straight line*. This incident does chime with that of the Freemans, but slightly out of tune. There are clear similarities - an odd couple, dressed in unfashionable clothes - but also differences. Are we dealing here with psychic rather than 'real' incidents?

A few days later, Gwen, on her way to the town centre to shop, bumped into Alison, one of her friends. For no obvious reason she could account for, an overwhelming compulsion to grasp and massage her friend's hands took control of her. She felt powerless to resist this unspoken order. Alison was clearly surprised by Gwen's gesture, but it was Gwen who, after a few seconds, broke contact as her normal shyness reasserted itself, colouring her face with embarrassment. She let go the hands with a few muttered words of apology. Both women were aware of an uneasy feeling as they parted.

Later Gwen wondered what her friend would think of her, and experienced a few qualms when Alison arrived at her door. Alison excitedly showed Gwen her hands. It turned out that she had suffered from arthritic fingers for several years. The stiffness had grown so pronounced that it was hard for her to hold any size of object. The attacks were painful into the bargain, with doctors managing little in the way of relief. Overnight, however, the pain and stiffness had gone. The 'miracle' had baffled the doctors, but they were forced to confirm the improvement. Alison felt sure that it was all down to Gwen's magic touch.

Gwen was relieved and delighted by Alison's news. Yet somehow it did not surprise her. It was almost as if she had known it was about to happen. The conviction grew inside her that the UFO incident, disturbing as it was, had left her with some form of healing ability.

It is difficult to estimate how often such encounters are followed by the development of this power to help others. In *Without Consent*, Carl Nagaitas and Philip Mantle describe in detail the case of Elsie Oakensen, who experienced a strange encounter which may have led to an alien abduction incident. In connection with the Freeman case, however, the interesting aspect is that Elsie became a healer, which, she believes, was as a direct result of her UFO encounter. This ability was of such significance that Elsie, in fact, became a member of the National Federation of Spiritual Healers. Similarly to Gwen Freeman, Elsie Oakensen viewed her encounter as having a strong spiritual element. The interaction between the spiritual (or religious) aspects of UFO incidents and the 'alien' nature of the entities involved will be discussed in a later chapter. It is surely not a coincidence that in both Gwen's and Elsie's cases a white beam of light played a significant part in the experience. Elsie consciously recalls 'a brilliant circle of pure white light' appearing close by the sides, rear and front of the car. Under hypnosis she said, 'A brilliant white light is shining in my eyes ...' The light seemed to suffuse her whole body. Of course, there are aspects of the encounter which distinguish it from Gwen Freeman's. Gwen, apparently, did not undergo an abduction experience, but as so often happens, the similarities between cases tantalise the mind without offering any solution to the UFO enigma.

Gwen herself had enjoyed good health, as Sid himself described to me during my visit to the bungalow. A few weeks before the sighting she had gone through a medical check, including a cardiograph, prior to a minor operation. Everything was normal. Sid, however, took the view that soon after these April events, his mother's health began to deteriorate. It was a gradual process spread over some months. In April 1987 Gwen Freeman developed a sudden illness and in November unfortunately died of a heart attack. Sid senior is convinced that his wife's encounter led directly, in some uncertain yet tragic way, to her early death.

One of the paradoxes of this case is that the UFO incident was witnessed by Gwen rather than Sid junior, when it might have been expected that the opposite would have been the case.

There is no doubt that Sid is psychic, testified to by the fact that he had experienced strange phenomena from an early age. On the other hand, it is noticeable that Gwen, prior to 1984, had not been an obvious channel for any paranormal phenomenon. When Sid was hospitalised at seven years old with a kidney disorder, he felt compelled one day to get out of bed and look out of the window. He immediately became aware of a blinding light and, as if in a trance, stared into the heart of the glowing object. According to Sid, in spite of having suffered badly through illness, his health immediately improved and he was 'miraculously' cured.

It is noticeable that a bright light appears in Sid's and Gwen's encounters, although with opposite effect. Sid's poor health is improved, a direct beneficial effect on him, whereas Gwen Freeman is given the ability to help others, with possibly adverse results for her own wellbeing.

Sid experienced at least one more strange incident after the UFO encounter. One evening he watched a flaming ball of fire hurtle over the night sky, coming from a northerly direction. Sid described it to me as being as 'big as five houses' and followed its path with awe as it headed at tremendous speed for the nearby Sidlaw Hills. He felt sure, given its trajectory, that it must crash into one or other of the summits, as it definitely seemed to be heading towards solid ground. He waited for signs of the expected impact, but nothing happened. After some minutes, he guessed that the object had been travelling much higher than he had thought.

This event took place in early 1990 and, unless there was a particular piece of space debris crash landing at that time, Sid must have gone through some kind of psychic vision. Anything as large as Sid claimed to have seen would surely have made newspaper headlines, but we can find no report that fits Sid's description.

Sid looks every inch the sensitive artist: tall, thin, a quiet air, but occasionally revealing a hidden intensity. You might expect Sid to experience psychic phenomena even if you didn't know that he had. And though anyone can possess psychic ability, Mrs Freeman, from her photos a pleasant, comfortable looking woman, looks the opposite of the traditional view of a medium. Even so, it seems more than likely that Sid inherited his ability from his mother, but hers lay dormant until that fateful day when a strange encounter brought it into action.

On its own, the Freeman encounter entitles Blairgowrie to be considered a UFO hot spot ('UFO Capital of Scotland', as the *Scottish Sunday Mail* headlined it in its 19 January 1991 issue). The truth, though, is proverbially stranger than fiction and this certainly holds for this isolated part of Scotland. There is something odd occurring in this small area of the country: crop circles; balls of light; cattle mutilations; and UFOs. All making an appearance within much less than an ordinary square mile.

To show the odd way coincidence works, my attention was first drawn to Blairgowrie not by a UFO, but by Scotland's first confirmed crop circle. This had appeared in June 1990 on the very fringe of the town in a field of grass bordering the A923 and owned by the Ardblair estate. Unfortunately, the appearance of this phenomenon only came to my attention in late July, and by the time I journeyed to inspect it the owner, Laurence Oliphant, had already harvested the field.

There were, in fact, as it turned out, two circles. With the assistance of paranormal investigator Malcolm Robinson, and using dowsing techniques, we were able to locate the position of the circles and take measurements. At this late stage it was not possible, of course, to be exact. For the record, however, this is what we found: the upper circle was 71 feet in diameter, but the lower circle was only half that size at 36 feet across. Both circles had been formed at the west edge of the field beside a thick clump of trees which overhung the edge of a disused stone quarry. The field itself covered almost the full slope of the hill on which it stood. The formation we went to investigate had been created about one third of the way up. Avoiding the grazing sheep, I tested the site with dowsing rods and was surprised by the powerful response which set the metal sticks juddering in my fists. The existence of an unknown, yet 'natural', energy source might be a clue to explain the circle phenomenon. UFO investigator

Ken Higgins, however, with whom I later visited the site, remained doubtful and wanted to know how the two were connected. If only there was an answer! All I could do was to point out that the area surrounding the two sworls was criss-crossed by lines of energy which ran in both south/north and east/west directions. There was something strange in this field, even if for the moment I couldn't explain it.

I was not, of course, trying to connect the Freemans' UFO sighting with the two circles as several years separated these events. However, it is not perhaps without significance that the rare appearance of crop circles in Scotland should occur near a town with one of the strangest UFO encounters ever recorded.

Interestingly, it has been alleged that cattle died in mysterious circumstances in the same field close to the time that the crop circles were formed. According to our informant (who does not wish to be identified) the necks of cattle loose in the field were found broken, with no explanation of how this could have occurred. We have been unable to confirm that these incidents took place.

Returning with Ken Higgins to the A923 at the point where it exited Blairgowrie and bordered the crop circle field, we drove on to Ardblair Castle to meet Laurence Oliphant, owner of the area and descendent of the same Oliphant who fought alongside Bonnie Prince Charlie in the '45 war. History comes to life in Scotland. Mr Oliphant showed us where a spectacular ley transected his ancestral home, confirming our view that the whole area was one tremendous mystery. But could it (if it did) explain the UFO sightings?

In fact, at this stage I had no idea that any significant UFO sightings had occurred in Blairgowrie. While Ken and I were speaking over the car 'phone some months earlier, he mentioned something about a lady having seen a light in the sky in the village. It sounded interesting, although not particularly attention grabbing. We agreed to make an appointment to visit and it was left to Ken to make the arrangements. It turned out later that Ken had tried to agree a date for our visit, but for various reasons no date had proved suitable. As the weeks rolled by, the incident faded from memory as UFO reports of more recent sightings rolled in.

Now, admiring the towering walls of Ardblair Castle from its surrounding gardens, Blairgowrie's UFO encounters had completely disappeared from our minds. A comment made by one of the Oliphant family, however, started a little cog moving. It seemed that strange balls of light had been seen in the vicinity and their appearance coincided with the paths of energy lines - or leys - on the estate. I had dowsed one myself in the shadow of the castle. The little cog, however, took a while to turn. About a week later, on the way home from work, the faint recollection of past conversations began to gather strength. Reaching the drive, I fairly dived into the hall to grab the 'phone.

'Didn't you tell me about a UFO incident in Blairgowrie?' I barked at an astonished Ken.

'Which one do you mean?' responded Ken, who appeared remarkably calm in response to my abrupt question.

It was my turn to be taken aback.

'You mean there were more than one?' I said in amazement.

As quickly as he could, Ken told me of various incidents he had uncovered during the past week. And how he had attempted to make contact with the Freeman family while driving through the area, but been unable to do so. In my turn, I reminded Ken about the crop circles and strange lights. For a moment we fell silent. It was clear that we had uncovered a remarkable series of events in what appeared on the surface to be a rather unremarkable town. Spurred on by these surprising discoveries we uncovered through diligent investigation a whole series of UFO incidents spanning an incredible thirty year period.

In October 1957, at around seven in the morning, a nurse cycling over the Ericht Bridge observed a metal disc hovering over the road bordering the river. This was, in fact, Riverside Road, that same street into which the Freemans were later to move from England and experience their strange encounter. The nurse at the time claimed to have heard a soft humming and estimated the object to be thirty feet in diameter. It 'hung in the sky', as she described it, before disappearing in a northerly direction. Significantly, perhaps, she noted that as it moved it followed the course of the river. It may be coincidence, but it is nonetheless fact, that the flow of the Ericht through Blairgowrie follows a well known fault line. Was this of some strange interest to the UFO?

Exactly two months to the day after the Freemans' encounter, another UFO was sighted over Blairgowrie. There were four witnesses to this event, including a mother and son. None of those who saw the phenomenon, however, wishes to have their identity revealed. The date was 25 June 1984. The time, 9.30 in the evening. The object appeared at first in the distance as a bright circle about the size of a tennis ball, and trailing a red tail. Every so often a beam of light flashed from its circumference. At the same time, although only visible through binoculars, a strange V shaped object was seen to leave and then return to the 'tennis ball'. This manoeuvre was gone through several times. After a while both objects seemed to disappear into the sky.

The witnesses were so intrigued by the experience that they met up with the Freemans to compare notes. Both families had been left in a state of mystery by their out-of-the-world encounters and were desperate to find a solution to these strange events. A solution, however, was not readily to hand.

Having observed Blairgowrie from a distance, it seems that the UFO decided the time had arrived to take a closer look. A businessman on a skiing holiday claimed that he and his wife were followed by a disc-shaped object for four miles along the Glenshee road, just to the north of Blairgowrie. As the couple drew near to some houses, the UFO, still glistening brightly, shot skywards and disappeared at tremendous speed. It was as if it did not like being observed and had made a fast exit before the holidaymakers had time to draw others' attention to it.

Over the following months, Blairgowrie continued to be plagued by weird phenomena. One mile to the west of the town lies the freshwater Loch of Rae. Several residents, who do not wish to be named, reported to Ken Higgins that they had witnessed on a number of separate occasions yellow and white lights moving erratically across the surface of the loch. Local lore has it that sightings of strange glowing objects have been noted since at least the 1960s and, it might be suspected, for a good while before then.

Earth mystery investigators have pointed out that the local countryside is rich in ancient artifacts. Standing stones, neolithic monuments and pictish carvings testify to a long history of habitation. The area was strangely attractive to prehistoric man, who responded by decorating the land with these enigmatic messages to posterity. The enigma continues today with sightings of UFOs which find the area as attractive as did our forebears.

UFOs may have put Blairgowrie on the map, but Perthshire is dominated by the city after which it is named. Perth has for long been the principal urban centre for the surrounding area, and was once the capital of medieval Scotland. It should come as no surprise, therefore, to learn that this ancient burgh in the modern age has also experienced UFO activity.

In 1985, a nurse crossing on foot the road bridge spanning the Tay was enveloped by a sudden silence. It was as if the space round about her had suddenly been blocked from the normal sounds of the world. This strange phenomenon is well known to UFO researchers (and labelled by top investigator Jenny Randles as 'the oz factor'). As she became accustomed to this strange experience, Anne, as we shall call her, slowly became aware of a presence hovering only a few yards in front of her. It was a translucent object about thirty to forty feet long, its shape broken by what seemed to be a window, although more like a viewing deck than a porthole.

Through the window Anne could make out several small entities. One of these creatures placed its hands over a number of levers which it seemed to be using to manoeuvre the craft around and above the bridge. After a short time, seconds only perhaps, the object moved away and vanished. Although it seemed to have lasted no length at all, the encounter left a vivid impression on Anne's mind. She had no difficulty in recalling the UFO's circular shape, as it appeared from where she watched, ending in a thin, streamlined tail at the rear. Anne was completely unaware of the Freeman sighting. All the more remarkable, then, that her description should correspond so closely with the Blairgowrie UFO.

When Anne 'came to' she was shocked to realise that pedestrians passing within feet of her had not witnessed the incident which was so real to her. Incredibly, in broad daylight, on a busy thoroughfare, she had been the sole observer of what to all intents and purposes seemed like an extra-terrestrial spacecraft. Anne called out to a passing cyclist, for the 'craft' had reappeared just a few yards away! It was shifting, but only slowly, making no sound as it moved stealthily beside the river. A thousand tangled thoughts rushed through Anne's mind. Was it trying to contact her? Was it searching for something? Trying to abduct someone? Looking for somewhere to land? Anne felt no fear, only an overwhelming desire to learn more of what these unusual visitors were up to. Unfortunately, time was fast running out for Anne. Once again the object's slow movements were taking it gradually out of her sight. Then it was gone; this time for good.

At the moment the UFO disappeared all daily sounds came flooding back in an overwhelming burst of consciousness. The roaring of passing cars, thud of feet on pavements and chatter of fellow pedestrians. Anne's world returned to normal, or as close as was possible after such an experience. But as Anne freely admits, her life could never be the same again. Anne has been on the receiving end of several strange experiences since that encounter. Though no longer in the Perth area, she went through a bizarre incident involving humanoid type entities on a train journey over the Forth Railway Bridge. These entities claimed that they lived under the very Forth Estuary over which they were travelling. The nature of Anne's experience points to some type of psychic awareness being activated, as if a viewing slot to another dimension was being opened.

Karen's encounters, however, may point in a different direction. These had their origin in 1976, almost a decade before Anne's encounter in Perth. And unlike Anne, Karen was many miles away from the city when she stumbled across a most strange sight. Karen was ten years old at the time, living with her family in a farm cottage close to the village of Meigle. Yes, that very centre of the 'mysterious north', with its vast collection of standing stones and their still undeciphered script. If there is one area in Scotland where you might anticipate a strange encounter, it is surely the countryside lying between the River Island and the Loch of

Lintrathen. Beautiful, remote, isolated. To a child, however, the land about is simply home, a place to run and play in. So it was for Karen. In the summer of 1976, Karen was recovering from mumps and stayed in the cottage while her brothers and sisters went out fruit picking, a traditional occupation in the area at this season of the year. She had decided instead to go to a nearby wood, taking a picnic with her. She set off from the old farm cottage at around 9.45 a.m. and arrived at the wood half an hour later, just after ten o'clock. During the walk to the wood she watched a bright rainbow coloured light in the sky, although any connection with what was shortly to take place is unproven.

Having entered the wood, Karen walked down familiar paths until she came to a clearing well known to her. Later, much later, as she thought back on the events of the day, she remembered that she had been struck by a strange silence that enveloped her as she made her journey. All bird and animal noises had stopped. The only sound that echoed through the silent wood came from the dry earth crunching beneath her feet.

Now even that had been muffled into silence. But it was not out of choice that she still stayed at her favourite picnic spot. Karen admits that she would have turned and run if she had been given the opportunity. Unfortunately, she didn't have the option. Ahead of her, staring at her, were a group of little figures, four in all, and she, confronted by this strange group, was unable to move. She was, she says, 'frozen to the spot'.

The entities started to come towards her and as they did so she could see that not only their eyes but, more remarkably, their skin was coloured blue. They were small, smaller even than 10 year old Karen, probably not even topping her shoulder.

And then she felt hands touching her, cold and slimy. An enormous light appeared from nowhere and the next thing that Karen can picture is lying on a big circular table which had the appearance of hard metal, but felt soft around her, almost as if it had been moulded to the contours of her body. Entities surrounded her, telling her everything was all right. Not a word, though, was spoken. It all happened through thoughts that came into her mind. These beings looked human, but she also caught sight of taller entities whose bodies were incredibly thin, like stick insects.

She believes that the small entities she first encountered may have been working for these taller aliens.

The place she was in was dark, but she remembers a light shining from somewhere. Drops were put into her eyes which paralysed them for a while. Clearly some form of examination was underway as Karen recalls a 'contraption like a machine' covering her from head to toe and going into her mouth. It may have examined her nostrils as well.

Eventually, Karen was returned to the spot where her mysterious journey had begun. Dazed and shaken, she headed for home. When she walked in, a further shock was sprung on her. She was sure she had been in the woods only a short time. It couldn't be later than lunch time. In fact, it was 6 p.m., way past the usual time for her evening meal. It had been over eight hours since she had waved goodbye and set off with her picnic. Her frantic parents had been on the point of calling the police.

For the next two years, Karen avoided the woods. But in 1978 she experienced a second encounter. The night before the incident Karen had a vivid dream in which she went back to the scene of the first incident and found the small figures waiting for her. It seems that the dream somehow propelled her back into her old haunts. She returned to the picnic site and was once again 'taken up' by the strange entities. She could feel their little hands touching her legs, lifting her as if she was being guided somewhere. She remembers lying on a table and experiencing an agonizing pain centred on her forehead.

Back home she suffered a headache and a high fever and was violently sick during the night. A doctor visited and she remembers him saying that her glands were inflamed.

Once again Karen may have suffered a period of 'missing time'. She left home around midday and returned around four o'clock. Not, perhaps, an unusual length of time for a child to be out playing, but Karen feels that the incident she experienced could not possibly have filled that four hour gap. What happened during that period? Karen as much as anyone would like the answer.

Until recently, she made no attempt to find one and buried the experience deeply within the recesses of her memory. She told no one of her encounters. Her parents and brothers and sisters were wholly unaware of the incidents. For almost twenty years Karen said nothing. By 1995 she had moved to a large city and had a small child. Memories of her encounter began to surface in her dreams, with the worrying feeling that these entities might have a particular interest in her daughter. She felt a compulsion to return to the very spot in the wood where the beings had appeared to her. Karen even drove part of the way there before turning back. Karen did experience another 'missing time' incident. This time it occurred in her own home.

She was doing some late studying in the back room of the flat, which doubled as her daughter's bedroom. She remembers seeing a bright light coming in through the window. In the light she recalls catching sight of a dog-faced entity. When she 'came to' an hour had passed. The coffee she had been drinking had gone cold. Karen had no conscious memory of being abducted, but naturally fears that such an event might have taken place.

What are we, as observers, to make of the strange dog-faced entity? What possible link could there be with unidentified flying objects? Or abduction cases? On the surface, it may seem that there is no link, that the vision experienced by Karen does not gel with her other encounters. However, I would suggest that is far from being true, and that this incident can be seen as central to the UFO phenomenon.

The link I am going to make may seem at first far fetched, but I would ask the reader to bear with me. It is not simply a device to shock.

The dog-faced entity was well known to ancient Egypt. He was known as the god Anubis. Certainly, Anubis was normally represented with the head of a jackal, and the body of a man, but in some instances he was sculpted with a dog's face. Anyway, at a glance a dog's head looks much like that of a jackal. I would suggest, therefore, that it was this being that Karen saw at the time.

It is not, however, my intention to list the attributes of Anubis, or explain how he was regarded in ancient Egypt. He was, for example, seen as the personification of the summer solstice, the protector of Osiris and the guardian to the dead in the underworld. All these aspects may have had some significance in his appearance to Karen, but if so then the connection is not at the time of writing an obvious one to me. I believe that the incident was a general indication to Karen of a link between ancient Egypt and a present day mystery: the wonder of UFOs. From recent research, some of which has reached the general public with bestsellers such as *Fingerprints of the Gods* and *The Orion Mystery*, it is clear that ancient Egypt was a much older civilisation than can be imagined and also possessed a deeper knowledge of the mysteries of the universe. And one of these mysteries was possibly contact with alien civilisations. Why Karen has been singled out for that experience, it is impossible to say, but as time passes the meaning of this experience for Karen herself may become clearer.

To anyone who might think that she is imagining things, Karen can point to the discovery of a strange object in her gums, confirmed by X-ray. She has visited a specialist who has definitely indicated that an unidentifiable object which looks hard and metallic is located in her mouth. Karen was completely unaware of this object until it was noticed by her dentist. It caused her no discomfort and how it found its way there is a complete mystery. Medical investigation into the matter continues and it would be wrong to classify this as an 'alien implant' as there is no evidence which can point in that direction, as yet.

It may be relevant to note that less than thirty miles from the area of Karen's encounters lies Aberfoyle, home to the Reverend Robert Kirk, the seventeenth century church minster who accepted entities from the 'other side' as a normal part of life. His favourite meeting place was at a spot now called the 'Fairy Knowe' (or hill), a mile or so from the present town. From his own experience and those he gathered from acquaintances, Kirk compiled a dossier of these beings from other worlds which he published under the title *The Secret Commonwealth* in 1692. The beings described by Kirk were very much part of the woods and hills of the time (and, of course, in such an environment Karen experienced her encounter). These entities also seem to have some of the abilities we associate today with alien entities. They could, according to Kirk, make their bodies 'appear and disappear at pleasure' and 'enter houses' at will. They are like us in appearance, but can take on other shapes if they want to in order to confuse or impress humans. These entities do possess weapons which 'somewhat of the nature of a thunder-bolt subtely and mortally wound the vital parts without breaking the skin'. The comparison between Kirk's denizens and present day alien entities should not be drawn too closely. There are probably as many differences as similarities, but there does appear to be a connection of some kind, although as with so much in the world of ufology, the exact relationship appears intangible. However, the blue colour of the beings Karen confronted, a feature which makes a difficult story even harder to accept, was, in fact, a colour traditionally associated in Scotland with the 'other people' of the woods. Stranger still, in the context of Karen's later experience, is that the colour blue was also that of the clothes worn by the Pharaohs, rulers of ancient Egypt, a fact of which Karen was completely unaware until I informed her and of which I was ignorant until I researched her strange mixture of experiences.

THREE

A MAP OF MYSTERY

Lying in rough seas off the northernmost tip of Scotland, Orkney and Shetland have a reputation for isolation which even the twentieth century has not wholly washed away. From the ruins of Skara Brae to the freezing grandeur of ancient Jarlshoff, the islands are haunted by memories of a past which impinges more vividly here than in the tourist-wracked grandeur of Stonehenge. Yet in spite of the well known Up-Helly-A festival with its primitive pagan imagery, times have moved forward as elsewhere. In the 1990s the islands are part of a cosmopolitan culture which plays to a similar agenda the world over. The discovery of oil has changed all, and UFO sightings occur as frequently, if not more so, as in the rest of the United Kingdom.

The proof that UFOs know no geographical boundaries is shown in the experience of Arthur Moar, an inhabitant of Sandwick, one of the remoter parts of the remote Shetland Isles. A retired small-farmer, Mr Moar was used to early rising and Monday morning 6 January 1992 was no different from any other day until five minutes past seven arrived. He could be sure of the time as he had just finished checking the dial on the clock. All thoughts, however, of continuing with his daily routine were disturbed by the appearance of a bright, flashing light which lit up the whole room. Mr Moar hurried to the window and observed a strange object standing on the ground about 30 or 40 yards from his house. Perhaps 'strange' in this case is an understatement. 'Bizarre' does not even rise to the occasion. A description in Mr Moar's own restrained words says a lot about his ability to remain unruffled! The object, he reported, 'was about five or six feet high with flame all around it' and 'in the centre I saw the globe of the world and ... all the markings on the globe'.

A flaming globe landing from the sky! It is without doubt one of the most incredible sightings ever. Mr Moar noted that the globe was grey coloured and that the area round the globe was dark red. The object was enclosed by a flange about 4 inches across. From the rear of the object protruded a round, white tube, out of which flashed the intense light which had first caught Mr Moar's attention.

The globe, he adds, was of suede-like material and even appeared to have rumpled up in the manner of a hastily dumped coat. Even as he watched, the UFO flew up into the air, leaving behind the white tube which remained standing on the ground. This tube, which to all intents and purposes looked solid, gradually faded away until it eventually disappeared from view. Although Mr Moar observed the object for only a short time, it is an event he is unlikely ever to forget.

On a scale of strange events listing from 1 to 10, I would classify this as a definite number 10. Why? Because there seems no obvious object in the first place which could provide a justification for claiming a misidentification and secondly, the UFO did not look remotely like a 'flying saucer'. Why on earth would ET choose to land on Shetland or anywhere else in a globe of the world, covered in suede and enveloped in flame? If it wasn't from outer space, what on earth was it? If further reports are received of a similar object we will, perhaps, be in a better position to find a solution.

Less dramatically, perhaps, but equally intriguing, the Shetlands too have been plagued by a variety of mystery lights. In December 1992 dozens of callers bombarded the police, and anyone in authority, with reported sightings of a fire ball streaking across the night sky, travelling from north west to south east. Other witnesses who contacted Lerwick coastguards described it as a 'bright white light', but it was undoubtedly the same object. Checks with the RAF base at Pitreavie Castle drew a blank. Officially, there were no planes in the area at the time. The phenomenon may have been the same as that seen further south on the mainland by Alistair Donaldson out walking his dog in Banchory around 8.50 p.m. He reported it as being 'as bright as a star', with 'sparks coming out of the back, and it had a tail. There was no noise'. He explained that he did not believe in UFOs, but that it definitely was not an aeroplane or a helicopter.

Not to be outdone by their island compatriots, the inhabitants of Orkney have their own strange tales to tell. One January morning in 1994 Stephen Leech of Stenness (close to the famous standing stones of Broghar) was travelling to work with colleague Paul Anderson. They were heading along the A965 to the island's main city, Kirkwall. Suddenly, 45 year old Steve, a native of Yorkshire, spotted a 'huge, glowing, cigar-shaped object' travelling across the sky at a fantastic speed. Steve noted that 'it was gone in a couple of seconds and was moving too fast for an aeroplane'. Although it was 8.30 in the morning with a cloudy sky, both men were convinced of what they had witnessed, even noting the turquoise colour of the object. Steve and Paul came forward with reluctance to give their account, but felt sure that with all the traffic on the road that morning other car drivers must have seen the strange object. As is often the case, however, they were disappointed by the lack of corroborative responses.

Did the object head out to sea? Surrounded by water, it would be reasonable to assume that the object must have crossed the shoreline at some point. Not surprisingly in view of the volume of UFO sightings, encounters in the North Sea fishing lanes are not unusual. Some years ago a trawler from Aberdeen, the *Avondee*, was hauling in a catch near the Bell Rock about thirty miles from the coast. It was around 11 p.m. on a typical summer's night in June. The ship's cook, Mr James Blackhall, was looking at the stars when his attention was caught by two orange-red objects moving at tremendous speed. He pointed out the strange phenomenon to Samuel Noble, whose turn it was to take the watch, and shouted to the rest of the crew, 'Come and see the flying saucers!'

This was clearly jumping to conclusions although they had obviously spotted something out of the ordinary. It is hard, for example, to judge from the account the objects' height above the sea. Mr Blackhall estimated their size in the sky from his location as about 3 inches high and 3 feet broad. But that does not tell us whether they were very large objects at a high altitude or smaller objects near to the trawler. UFOs of all shapes and sizes have been encountered even up to a mile in length! Mr Blackhall explained that, 'At first they seemed to be moving together, but suddenly sheered off and disappeared'. The UFOs left behind a luminous trail, but, unlike a conventional jet, when the object disappeared the trail disappeared instantly as if it had been swallowed by a black hole.

The crew kept watching in hope that the mysterious visitors would reappear, but the sky remained empty. Perhaps the final word should be given to the *Avondee*'s skipper who was the last on deck when the cry 'flying saucer' was heard. 'When I arrived,' he explained, 'there was only one object. It was like a ball of fire'. Balls of fire moving as if under intelligent control. What can it mean for the nature of a universe we too often take for granted?

Perhaps the skipper of the *Avondee*, however, would have been relieved to learn, if he'd been able to jump ahead in time, that he would not be the last sailor to witness a close encounter. On 22 November 1963, the crew of the fishing boat *Collier*, plying in the Girdleness area of the North Sea, were startled by a bright red light which swooped down from a clear sky and plunged into the sea close by their ship. So convincing was the event that the witnesses were sure they had seen a crash of some kind and immediately launched a search for possible plane or helicopter wreckage. To close watchers of UFO phenomena it will come as no surprise to learn that they discovered neither dead bodies nor tangled wreckage. The surrounding water was clear of all evidence of a man-made disaster. Was this another example of the UFO-base-under-the-sea incident? It certainly will fuel those inclined to more extravagant explanations of UFO origins. It has to be said, however, that on this occasion at least, there is no suggestion from the witnesses that the object made anything like a controlled descent into the waves.

Those who go to sea in trawlers are familiar with lights and movements in the night sky which can strike the landlubber, used only to a cityscape, as decidedly odd. There are those, however, who scanning the sky during daytime or monitoring it with their radar sets can also be relied on to spot occurrences out of the ordinary. It is particularly striking when the witness in question is an air controller.

Andrew Duncan (a pseudonym, as for employment reasons the witness does not wish to be identified) was based at Dyce airport near Aberdeen. On 9 November 1991 (the anniversary of Bob Taylor's sighting!) at around 12.15 p.m., Mr Duncan was looking out of his operations' window when he spotted a strange object overhead. He put it in that category as, being used to seeing planes and helicopters from many different angles, he was unable to classify it with normal airport traffic. Fetching a pair of binoculars from the adjacent room, he focused on the UFO, but was still unable to identify it. Puzzled, Mr Duncan called up Air Traffic Control (ATC) and asked, 'What on earth is that?' From the tower, however, the men could not see the object which appeared clearly visible to Duncan. ATC informed him that they would contact radar and get back to him as soon as possible.

Meanwhile, a light aircraft had appeared on the airport circuit, but gave no indication by way of message or evasive action that it was aware of its mysterious companion. Mr Duncan called two colleagues through, but by the time they had got it within their sights the UFO looked considerably smaller and they were unable to make an identification. They had, however, definitely seen 'something'. ATC now rang back and, to Mr Duncan's surprise, informed him that nothing had appeared on radar. Glancing skywards again, he noted that the object was nowhere to be seen.

Overnight, Mr Duncan had time to consider the matter and by morning was still convinced that he had witnessed an intrusion which he could not easily explain. As a result, he decided to ring up Highland Radar at RAF Buchan near the fishing port of Peterhead. He was again surprised to learn that they had nothing logged for the time indicated. To Mr Duncan the incident remains an absorbing mystery. As he himself notes, 'I have a pretty in-depth knowledge of aircraft recognition ... and have always tried to keep up-to-date with ongoing developments. This object I can categorically state was not an aircraft'.

Nor does he believe that he witnessed something as 'ordinary' as a hot air balloon, as there was no 'visual sign of a basket suspended below the object and add to this the relatively light wind conditions and I think that you can rule this out'. If nothing else the shape of the object Mr Duncan saw would confirm this. How many balloons look like a cube, even at a distance? Cuboid UFOs are not unknown, but they do form the less familiar of the genre.

Interestingly, on 26 March of the same year at 11.20 a.m., a helicopter pilot on his way to Dyce airport picked up a highly visible trace on his radar screen. Surprised by its appearance, he checked on local shipping and aircraft movements to see if he could locate the source. He was unable, however, to make a positive identification. Mystified, the pilot formally notified Air Traffic Control of a UFO in the sky. ATC immediately informed the Ministry of Defence which rapidly scanned military air traffic to find out if one of its own transports was involved. Again, they drew a blank and, following standard procedure, fighter aircraft were scrambled to locate the intruder which could be anything from ET to a 'mundane' encroachment of UK air space by a Soviet reconnaissance plane.

Coincidentally, but maybe not, at around the time that the helicopter first spotted the UFO a loud bang shook the atmosphere over Aberdeen and was heard as far away as the town of Banchory, about 18 miles south west. Buildings apparently shook under the force of the explosion, and some witnesses claim to have seen flashes of light in the sky. Whether the UFO and the bang were in any way connected is uncertain except in one respect: no solution was discovered for either mystery.

It is comforting to confirm, however, that Aberdeen also experiences the green light phenomenon. A bright green light made several appearances during November 1992 on the outskirts of the city. Is the green glow only the visible manifestation of a much larger object? In the nearby town of Alford, four boys caught sight of a large saucer-shape, as big as a double-decker 'bus across its width. The 'saucer' was itself grey coloured, but exhibited red, purple and green lights.

Far from being afraid, the boys ran towards the object, which took off at great speed. Over excited imagination? It might be thought so, if it wasn't for the fact that on the following day, 3 December 1992, again in Alford, a witness saw a large disc-shaped object hover over a nearby hill for several minutes before heading on a southwards trail.

Interestingly, a decade earlier, a similar object, though this time described as ambulance sized, was seen in Banff. It hovered above a house and a band of red and green lights around its circumference was clearly visible. After a few minutes the object moved away.

People often see bright lights whose source they cannot explain, but occasionally bright lights seem to single out witnesses.

On 16 December 1990, two bakers on their way to work were approaching the Kessock Bridge over the Beauly Firth when a bright light lit up the interior of their car. It appeared as a direct beam as if searching them out deliberately for attention. The witnesses were so startled by the abrupt transformation of night into day that the driver brought the car to a sudden halt. The beam of light immediately disappeared. The two men took the opportunity to have a good look around. They could see nothing that could provide a solution to the strange phenomenon, either on the ground or in the sky.

Around the same time, a family travelling in a car between Inverbervie and Stonehaven on Scotland's north east coast experienced a similar event. A pencil of light suddenly emerged from the sky and penetrated the interior of the car. The incident was over in seconds, but left the family puzzled and curious. There was no obvious source for the light. It seemed to come out of nothing. The family, however, had been aware of a mysterious light dancing in a nearby wood as they passed through, though there is no evidence that these two incidents were in any way connected.

Strange beams of light coming from nowhere to land on the earth are a phenomenon known to ufologists from all over the country. In Kinross, for example, during August 1982, a witness saw a bright beam of light descend from the sky. However, in contrast to the cases described above, he also caught sight of a bright object which seemed to be the light source. It may be that on each occasion the light beam is encountered it is, in fact, being projected from an object in the sky, but that witnesses are not always fortunate enough to catch a glimpse of it.

If light beams are sent by extraterrestrials' spaceships, do they land and do creatures then emerge to walk the earth? A lot of 'ifs' and 'buts' are wrapped up in that possibility! And unfortunately or not, there are surprisingly few cases in Scotland to suggest the reality of ET, whether as 'monster' or humanoid (human like).

One that certainly stretches the imagination occurred in Braemar, near Balmoral, the queen's residence in Scotland. The Territorial Army (TA) were holding a weekend training session and had based their headquarters close to the village of Tarland, about an hour's drive from Aberdeen.

Manoeuvres for the night having been arranged, two of the party were left to guard a hilltop with orders to dig a trench as part of the exercise. It could not have been a comfortable assignment on a cold November night with little to do except watch the movement of the stars. It was with understandable relief, then, that they watched the first glow of the sun emerging above the mountain tops. It also marked the start of a truly bizarre experience.

The soldiers heard, at first, a strange gurgling noise which seemed to come from a clump of trees a few hundred yards from their temporary base. At this point the apprentice recruits felt no sense of fear and were merely curious, glad of some relief from a night of cold and boredom. They set off to investigate, walking towards the silhouetted pines. Suddenly, out of the lessening gloom, two large figures emerged and headed in a stumbling manner towards them.

The creatures' size, seven to eight feet tall they later judged, coupled with their strange movements and incessant gurgling, petrified the TA's finest. They managed to note, however, that the strange noises coming from the two 'spacemen' were, in fact, their voices, strongly guttural in pronunciation. The creatures also seemed to be experiencing problems in traversing the countryside, as if they were either unsure of walking or, more imaginatively, unused to the earth's gravity.

The two soldiers did not stop to ask questions in their headlong retreat until they gained the safety of a hut a good distance away beside the main road. It was being used as a temporary shelter by Post Office engineers who were carrying out repair and improvement work. As they neared the hut, still running, they heard a swishing noise behind them. Turning, they saw all too clearly a brilliant glowing object, shaped like a disc, travelling fast up the road behind them. It was moving so quickly that there was clearly no escape.

Its appearance on the road, however, may have been pure coincidence and the 'terriers' involvement purely accidental as the UFO swooped over the men's heads, pulsating and leaving a shower of sparks in its wake. It soon disappeared from sight.

The soldiers now reached the safety of the hut and hammered loudly, battering fiercely on the door until they were let inside, where they poured out their unbelievable story.

Seasoned UFO watchers will feel a little uneasy over this encounter. It seems too exciting, with all the ingredients of a good SciFi story, particularly of that period. Though similar incidents have been reported from elsewhere in the world, an open mind on the incident might be the best attitude to adopt. My own efforts to locate the source of the story met with no success. The Aberdeen *Press & Journal* searched their archives, but could find no report of the incident.

It is true, however, that the mountains of Scotland have long been associated with the appearance of strange phenomena, from the ghostly grey man of Ben Macdhui to UFOs in the form of intense bright lights. It is the last type that has plagued the town of Fort William situated in the Western Highlands. One incident involved the owner of a hairdressing salon who with her husband saw a brilliant light on the top of Glen Nevis to the south of the town. Behind the glow they could make out the definite shape of a solid object. Although at some distance, it appeared to be round, orange coloured at the bottom with a flashing white light on top.

The couple had been watching a late TV film, so they could fix the time at around 1.30 in the morning. The object had been seen from their living room, but now they threw dressing gowns over their nightwear and, picking up binoculars, ventured outside to get a better look. The object had gradually moved towards the town and slowly passed overhead, allowing the couple an opportunity to inspect the underside with their field glasses.

They now had to modify their original impression of the shape. The underside appeared triangular, with panels through which orange light filtered down. The white light which had first attracted their attention could now more clearly be seen as a strip or panel on the side of the UFO, which itself now assumed a domed shape. The object was seen to be rotating as it moved.

The UFO travelled in an uncannily silent trajectory, emitting no noise whatever. Without warning, however, it accelerated in silence and shot northwest in a flash of light.

Subsequently, several witnesses to this UFO encounter appeared but, in spite of enquiries to RAF Lossiemouth and the local police, no obvious explanation has emerged. UFO sceptic and author Steuart Campbell has offered an explanation.

'It is possible', he wrote, 'that what was seen was a mirage of the star Antares caused by its light crossing a temperature inversion into an adjoining valley'. Although the impact of mirages should not be dismissed out of hand, and undoubtedly explains some UFO sightings, the proximity of the object makes it an unlikely source in this instance.

There is no more romantic setting in Scotland than that to be found in the Western Isles. It's the place every holidaymaker wants to visit at least once in his or her life. With its aura of mystery and still living legends, it's exactly the place you'd expect to find many UFO sightings if these encounters were simply the product of overactive imagination. It's interesting to note that, contrary to popular opinion, the Isles have been relatively free of such incidents. UFO investigator John Morrison, a native of the islands, believes that due to the natural reticence of the community many sightings go unreported. Everyone knows everyone else and in a close knit society it is too easy to become the butt of every budding comedian's jokes.

But when a report does surface, and even hits the local press, you know that something strange really has been going on. Or why else take the risk of raising your head above the parapet? The witness, described as a 25 year old shop assistant, watched the 'car sized fireball for ten minutes'. It was late on an August evening in 1995 as she travelled home from work. She described it as a 'huge orange oval' and was so fascinated by the fast moving object that, she says, she 'could not keep my eyes off it'. She first spotted the UFO as it approached from the west. It appeared to 'drop down and hovered some distance behind a group of houses before slowly rising up and then shooting across the sky at high speed'. Checks made by the *Stornoway Gazette* with local Air Traffic Control confirmed that there were no planes in the air at the time. The Meteorological Office denied that weather balloons were the cause of the sighting. However, contact with local fishing vessels around the Butt of Lewis at the time revealed no unusual sightings. The witness and her brother (who caught a fleeting glimpse of the object) were in no doubt of what they had seen. They were sure that others must have shared their experience. But being the Western Isles, fresh witnesses may well be cautious about stepping forward.

A wish for anonymity is understandable, particularly if you are a police officer. In the Spring 1996 edition of *Phenomenal News*, John Morrison described an intriguing incident which happened in late June or early July of 1993. 'Two local police officers saw two bright balls of light fly silently over their vehicle. They were bemused by the sighting and contacted the local airfield at Stornoway, who reported that there was 'nothing in the area'. A couple of days later Stornoway changed its mind and said there was 'an aircraft in the vicinity'. A very convenient discovery, one might conclude. Doubts about this explanation are given added fuel when, as Mr Morrison points out, you connect the policemen's sighting to an encounter which took place on 21 April of the same year. An Icelandair flight bound from Heathrow to Reykjavik was followed by two balls of light as it passed over the west coast of Scotland. One of these balls sat on each side of the tail plane all the way to Iceland. As the pilot made the final approach to Reykjavik, the two balls of light shot off to disappear into the horizon.

Some ufologists have linked the above incident to alleged confrontations with UFOs and USOs (unidentified submersible objects) in the North Sea. There have undoubtedly been many UFO sightings in that area, but no definite reports of hostile activity involving aliens and our own forces. However, those who believe that there is more going on in the seas around the North of Scotland no doubt feel that their position was fully justified by the events of October 1996. A mysterious incident which resulted in a full military alert, but has still to be satisfactorily explained. What is clear is that a massive explosion occurred off the Hebrides at 4.10 p.m. on Saturday 26 October. There were several witnesses to this spectacular incident from the sparsely populated area of the Butt of Lewis. Here's, however, where another mystery begins. According to the coastguard station in Stornoway (the island's main town), no calls were received from the public until 5 p.m., almost a full hour after the initial event. This is exactly the same time that, according to *UFO Magazine*, RAF Kinloss first heard reports of the incident. It appears to have been described as a possible aircrash with a large object (part of the fuselage) seen impacting with the sea. In spite of the report, the evidence is that there followed a two hour delay before an official air search was launched. It was not until 10.35 p.m. (six hours after the first witness called in) that an emergency message was broadcast to all ships within the vicinity, alerting them to the reported explosion.

It is true, and would have been noted at the time, that the description given by the witnesses did not tally in every detail. All the witnesses, though, did agree that there had been an enormous flash in the sky accompanied by a loud bang and a trail of smoke which led directly into the sea. Another witness claimed that just before the explosion he saw an object travelling high in the sky. When the detonation happened the object disappeared but a ball of smoke was clearly visible near the spot where he had last seen the UFO. The explosion was powerful enough to light up the sky in a bright orange flood.

Naturally, those who saw the incident felt that it must have been some kind of aeroplane accident. However, an extensive two day search involving coastguards and the massive, sophisticated resources of the military failed to find any evidence that an accident had occurred. That, of course, was the official verdict. As the military are secretive by nature, if there is an explanation it is unlikely to be revealed to the general public. This doesn't, of course, mean that we are dealing with a crashed extra-terrestrial spacecraft. However, the answer hinted at by the Ministry of Defence without, of course, being openly stated that a meteorite was involved, seems no more likely as an answer. This is particularly so as none of the chain of tracking stations across the Atlantic picked up this mysterious object, an admission which is astounding. How is it that an object big enough to produce a major explosion and be seen by at least one witness can enter NATO airspace without being tracked? There are clearly facts in this case which don't fully gel. If this mysterious object was not an extraterrestrial spacecraft, then what in the universe was it?

A variety of explanations were put forward as to the possible source of the explosion, but as investigators such as Tony Dodds of 'Quest International' and John Morrison of Scottish Earth Mysteries conducted their research, some puzzles were solved and new ones emerged. Was it coincidence, for example, that a major NATO exercise was held off the Isle of Lewis a week after the crash, on Monday 4 November? Did a weapon aboard a military aircraft accidentally arm itself and was it then jettisoned to avoid disaster? The substantial number of ships involved would have made it an ideal force to sweep the seas in the area for surviving debris. As might be expected, the military blandly claimed that it was a 'routine training exercise'. You don't have to be of a suspicious frame of mind to wonder whether that was the whole story. The military authorities are experts at concealing information they do not want the public to know. Secrecy is part of the system.

Several air to ground messages were also unearthed which seemed to indicate that a number of unidentified objects had been seen over the preceding months in April, July, August and as recently as 21 September. However, as John Morrison shows, not every 'mysterious' incident stays in that classification when looked at by a serious investigator. Considerable excitement was generated by an individual who had been listening to air traffic communications and reported the following comment:

Kinloss (air base): 'Confirm ... six feet long and three feet in diameter'. Clearly, military air traffic had received a report of an unidentified object seen in the vicinity at the time. Was this the source of the mysterious explosion? Unfortunately, it seems not. John Morrison discovered that further information revealed that a rescue helicopter had been despatched to look at the UFO. We know its exact position: 58.3 north 007.01 west. We also know the time it was first seen at 8.03 a.m. and the time it was reported as 'identified', at 8.10 a.m. According to the pilot of the helicopter, the strange object was simply a white cardboard box. Now, it might be asked, if the object was nothing more than a box, why did it take seven minutes to identify it? Furthermore, why were they spending time chasing objects in the sea in any case? The sea is full of floating debris. I would agree that these questions may have straightforward answers, but they are puzzles nevertheless.

One fact is unarguable. UFOs and the military have been known to each other for a very long time. On 21 March 1956 a little known, but very interesting, encounter took place involving a Sea-Hawk aircraft piloted by Sub-Lieutenant G W N Coates. The lieutenant was on a training flight, having taken off from HMS *Fulmar*, in the company of two other craft piloted by Lieutenant J Kelly and Sub-Lieutenant A Arundel from 738 Squadron. They had arrived off the coast of Lossiemouth at a height of 15,000 feet when Coates started filming with his camera. The weather was good with 'excellent visibility', the lieutenant explains. 'Being a novice, I had difficulty in keeping the graticules on the target, and I therefore don't think that I would have noticed anything at the edge of my field of vision'. In other words, no sighting of an airborne object was made at the time. However, 'When my film was developed and projected onto the screen, there was what appeared to be a perfect example of a flying saucer, moving on the port side ...'.

The sceptic, naturally, will immediately point to a straightforward explanation. However, as Coates pointed out, 'Theories that this was caused by the shadow of the sun have been discarded and I don't see how it could have been a blotch on the film'. He viewed the incident as 'most mysterious' and confirmed that the film had been 'sent to the Admiralty for official investigation'. His own views, he claimed, had considerably changed. 'Up to now I have not believed in the stories of flying saucers. Now I do not know what to think'. His colleagues on the flight appeared equally surprised. Lt Kelly commented, 'If there were such things as flying saucers, I believe it is conceivable that this is one'.

My efforts to trace this film were not successful. Nick Pope, then of the Ministry of Defence, informed me that all film from that date had long since disappeared. Of course, the event might be regarded as an elaborate hoax, except that the details given are quite specific. It certainly seems a well documented incident.

Phantom lights have been a phenomenon which has plagued the area around Muchalls near the fishing town of Stonehaven on Scotland's east coast. However, in an attempt to find a solution to these incidents and present the evidence investigator Tom McClintock has spent considerable time videoing activity there. What does the footage show? Certainly, there is something strange happening in the skies over this sparsely populated area. Round objects, gleaming balls of coloured light, dart about the sky in erratic movement or hang suspended in the air. Is that, you wonder, the propulsion of an unknown space vehicle, or the afterglow of a jet seen from an odd angle? The integrity of the investigator is beyond reproach and the evidence freely available for anyone to form an opinion.

It would be fair to say that the view of the majority of those who have reviewed the evidence and visited the area is that natural phenomena may explain the activity. The location is close to both aeroplane and, more significantly, helicopter routes. Dyce Airport, about fifteen miles north west, is the busiest helicopter base in Western Europe, with constant traffic to oil rigs drilling the North Sea floor. It is this regular movement which, it is argued, accounts for the alleged 'mysterious' light forms.

To counteract that, one must weigh the testimony of the investigator, a person with a responsible job who has everything to lose and nothing to gain by bringing forward his account. He has visited the area many times and holds the view that the source of these lights is not man made machines. If that is the case, then we are again at the very boundaries of the unexplained, with the opportunity of making a breakthrough, so frequently does the Muchalls phenomenon appear.

It is worth looking into the background of the key person involved and discovering what brought him to such an intense interest in the area's events. Tom McClintock's interest in strange phenomena began on 13 December 1971 when he returned to the village of Muchalls from his weekly violin lesson held in nearby Stonehaven. It was only a short journey from the bus stop to his house, but as he walked along he noticed a red pulsating light to his right. It was soon joined by an identical object to his left and then another appeared. Tom wasn't frightened by the three UFOs, only interested in trying to find out what they were doing. As he turned into the road that led directly to his home, events took a more disconcerting turn. One of the red lights came very low, almost to ground level. It caught Tom's attention for a moment, and he paused before moving forward. Just at that moment a strange figure appeared from nowhere standing right in the middle of the road. It was blocking Tom's path to his front door. The entity was dressed in a long gown and glowed brightly in the black evening of a rural setting. Showing amazing willpower for a young lad, Tom did not, as I suspect many of us might have done, turn and run or shout for help. Instead he moved a yard forward. The figure simply dissolved into nothingness.

Tom blurted out the story as soon as he got in the door and took his sister out to take a look. At first there was no sign of any strange light, but as they reached the end of the road, the red object appeared again. It came towards them without making any sound and hovered above their heads. Although they could make out a small ring of lights, no other details were visible. After a short time the UFO moved away to disappear over nearby hills.

What is particularly interesting and relevant is that Mr McClintock did not interpret this as simply a ghost incident, as might have been the case. Undoubtedly, it does have qualities that would point it in that direction. Even the appearance of odd lights do not mark it as definitely within the UFO ambit, as mysterious lights have long been associated with spectral encounters. However, that is not the way Tom saw it. In his mind it was within another category. In later years, Tom had other UFO sightings. In September 1988, for example, he again witnessed a pulsating red light, although this time he had a better look at the source. This was a flat topped object, drum shaped, with diamond facets on its circumference. It moved from behind a hill, and as it did so a white coloured halo appeared, flashed, then disappeared, as did the object itself behind a low cloud. As indicated, Tom McClintock has not only a story to tell, but hard evidence too. I find him a convincing witness.

Also situated on the east coast is a fishing village which must remain anonymous to protect our witness. Strange incidents have been plaguing her life. The woman in question, Jane Brown, is not a native of the area, but moved in many years ago, keen to escape the pressures of city life. She didn't come to the coast looking for alien encounters, but nor was she surprised when mysterious incidents started to happen. Jane had experienced alien contact from an early age and accepted the existence of extraterrestrials in much the same way as you and I would a visitor from a distant land. Different, but still a part of our world.

It's amazing how many people have had a UFO experience as a child. Jane falls into that category and it was while playing in the school grounds in Aberdeen that she spotted a silver, cigar shaped UFO travelling slowly in a cloud free sky. She was fascinated by the incident and felt that she wanted to learn more about distant worlds. But, of course, she was still a child and more immediate interests grabbed her attention. The UFO sighting faded into the background, although never completely lost from view.

Several years passed. Jane's family had moved to the south of England, living in a quiet housing estate. Jane had gone to bed, but a growing urge to look out of the window at the front of her house took hold of her. Jane got up and wandered into her brother's room as hers looked out the back. On the road outside, she saw a strange craft hovering a few feet above the ground. It was flat and circular, like a swollen pancake. The circumference was marked by a distinct band and within the band a series of lights were rotating. Jane recalls, 'I was excited. I ran downstairs and went outside. A humanoid alien was standing beside the craft. He was tall (almost six feet), dressed in a close fitting suit which also covered his hands and feet. He had a human build. I can't remember his facial features, but he looked human. I walked down the path towards him. He held out his hand, which I took and walked aboard the craft with him'. Jane said nothing to her family about this experience until almost fifteen years later.

In the 1990s Jane took up residence at her present address. Her house looks directly over a rocky foreshore, a tranquil view if the day is calm. But strange incidents have been taking place.

One night as Jane looked out of her bedroom window she saw a UFO come down above the high tide mark. Out of this craft strode five humanoid aliens. Jane felt that they had 'come back' for her. A wave of excitement raced over her. She ran downstairs, then opened the front door and raced down the garden path towards them. Thoughts of her children brought her to an abrupt halt. 'They'll be all right' went through her mind. Was this the aliens reassuring her? Wherever the thought had come from, she now felt sure everything would be all right. The leading alien was now level with her and stretched out his hand in greeting. 'He was', says Jane, 'exactly like the one' she'd seen all those years before. She took hold of his hand and allowed herself to be led towards the spacecraft. Then she felt herself standing at her living room window. The aliens and the UFO had both gone.

The incident was the start of a variety of strange incidents. One September, Jane was lying on the settee when several small aliens, between three and four feet tall, suddenly appeared. They had slits for mouths and black eyes like cats. Jane wanted to speak to these visitors, but found that she was unable to move. All around her everything went quiet. But Jane knew what the small entities were up to. She felt waves of light travelling through her, an experience she associated with scanning. The aliens turned her onto her stomach and continued to scan, if that is what they were doing. Jane emphasises that she felt no pain and had only a wish to communicate. Her visitors, however, seemed to have no desire to, or perhaps couldn't, respond.

Lights in the sky, or 'lits' as they are familiarly known, present an intriguing problem, but encounters which appear to involve extraterrestrials are bound to excite the imagination. Such a case occurred in the city of Elgin. At 6.30 p.m. on 18 May 1977, in the middle of a UK wide UFO flap, Mrs Caroline Maclennan heard a strange whirring noise and remarked to her neighbour that it sounded 'like a flying saucer'. Shortly after, her ten year old daughter Karen returned home and told Mrs Maclennan that she and her friend Fiona Morrison (also aged ten) had seen a 'silver coloured saucer with a bump on top' hovering in the wood. It had been close to the ground, glowing with a red light. Their attention had first been drawn to the object by a strange humming sound which seemed to have no obvious source. They were playing in fields close to the woods and it was from within the trees that the odd sound seemed to be coming. Being naturally curious, they decided to walk over and investigate. They quickly discovered the mysterious disc which they estimated at around 30 feet long. It seemed to be made of polished metal, but had no windows or doors that the girls could see. It had no identifiable marks either, although around the middle of the body section was a red rotating band.

The UFO was not sitting on the ground, but in the air at about a height parallel with a fence which separated the nearby housing estate from the wood. The estate, in fact, in which both girls lived. It should be borne in mind, however, that the witnesses were, by their own judgement, around 400 yards away and it is possible that the disc was standing on thin legs or some other supports which were hidden by trees or bushes in their line of sight.

It was at this point that the girls caught sight of a strange figure. It was dressed in silver, around six feet tall with short arms. The entity was standing close to the UFO, but they couldn't be sure if it was carrying out any activity, such as collecting objects, for example. The girls were disturbed by what they had seen, and when the figure seemed to move in their direction, they turned and ran. It soon became apparent after they had covered a short distance that they weren't being followed, so they stopped to look back. As they did so, the UFO moved in erratic motions to its left, before starting skywards at a tremendous speed. With that the girls returned home.

Mrs Maclennan took the girls' account seriously because she had herself been aware of the strange sounds, as had several of her neighbours. The police were informed, but didn't seem able to shed any light on the matter. The children were understandably reluctant to revisit the site, but the following day they plucked up the courage to go with Mrs Maclennan and take a look.

Around the spot where the UFO had been seen was an area about 100 yards across in which a large number of trees had apparently sustained minor damage, including scorch marks on the leaves. Grass had also been flattened. It is not known whether this part of the wood was compared to others, as trees suffer from all kinds of 'predators' from squirrels to high winds. The 'damage' may have been more apparent than real and simply coincidental. 'Scorching' on leaves, for example, may be confused with other natural effects. Soil samples were taken some months after the event, but the results of the analysis, if it was done, seem to have long since disappeared. It is doubtful whether they revealed anything of much consequence, as it's a safe bet that widespread publicity would have resulted from the discovery of significant anomalies. Bryan Hartly who investigated the case at the time was convinced of the sincerity of the witnesses and that they were being truthful about what they had seen. Several witnesses later came forward to claim they had observed a similar craft emitting a beam of light around the time of the girls' sighting.

Although Mrs Maclennan recently confirmed to me the substance of the report, the girls, now (of course) adults, had no wish to discuss the incident.

FOUR

A TALE OF TWO CITIES

On a bright summer day in 1978, a group of schoolchildren were distracted from playtime games by the strangest sight they were ever likely to see, even though they had the rest of their lives ahead of them. Hovering above the fence enclosing St Mark's Primary School in Muiryfauld, Glasgow, was an object which looked as if it had escaped from a Star Trek film. 'It glistened in the sun, about four feet across', recalls Euan Riley. 'It looked weird,' he remembers, a puzzled look in his eye, 'like two fedora hats joined together'. Then it just vanished. The incident was over too quickly for the pupils to summon any help. Would they have been believed anyway? 'Miss, there's a UFO outside the school!' Yet Euan's precise description is too keenly noted by a child's eye to be easily dismissed. It was silver coloured, he records, like shiny metal and very sharply defined, hovering about twenty feet above the ground. The sighting made a dramatic impact, so much so that Euan readily contacted SEMR when a case we had been investigating appeared in the popular *Glaswegian* newspaper, thanks to the interest of reporter Russell Findlay. Euan wrote, 'Although I was young, the memory of the incident has remained vivid in my memory, and I am sure of what I saw.'

Contact was made with the current head of St Mark's School, but so many years have passed no further information was available. Euan, however, was convinced that there had been other witnesses to the event though he could not remember the names of anyone present and was reluctant to carry out his own investigation as he still lived within the locality.

By an odd coincidence one of Scotland's earliest recorded UFO sightings also took place in Glasgow, and involved a school.

In 1952 Joan Torrence was leaving Elder Park Primary with her friends. It was 4 p.m., the end of the school day, and a warm summer's evening lay ahead of them. As Joan crossed the playground, a dark shadow stamped itself across the school. The sun had disappeared from sight. She looked up as did a swarm of pupils who seconds before had all been heading cheerfully for home. What Joan saw brought her to an abrupt halt and has been burned into her mind ever since. About a hundred feet up, a little above the school steeple, hung a sombrero shaped object, tilted slightly to one side. It seemed to be rotating. Joan watched for she doesn't know how long, but aware that her teacher, a step behind, the janitor on one side and her friend on the other were also entranced by the mysterious object. 'Time seemed to stand still', explained Joan. The spell was broken by the sudden movement of the UFO, preceded by a distinct whining sound. It shot off, heading across Glasgow to be seen and reported by other witnesses. Joan ran home to tell her mother what she had seen. A disbelieving parent had to eat her words when she read the reports in the following day's papers!

A surprising fact is that the Glasgow conurbation, in spite of having about double Edinburgh's population, has easily less than half the number of UFO incidents compared with those reported around the capital. Why is Glasgow less popular than Edinburgh for such encounters? There seems no obvious explanation for this imbalance. Both cities, for example, have airports close by and this fact alone, you might think, could lead to misidentifications of plane lights and result in UFO reports. The debunkers would gladly explain UFO incidents over the Lothians as aircraft tracking in to land, but the comparison with Glasgow seems to lead to the conclusion that such trite 'solutions' do not hold good. If mistaking aircraft for UFOs was the only answer, Glasgow - a busier airport - would surely with its greater population produce more sightings. The opposite, in fact, is true. Edinburgh has double Glasgow's close encounters.

Several of the Glasgow cases, however, provide good evidence that unexplained encounters are a reality which cannot be dismissed. In May 1976, Allistair McNeil, now a 44 year old actor, was sitting in a flat in Westbourne Gardens whiling away the hours in social chat with two friends Amanda Ross and John Dunn. Glancing occasionally at the clock, Allistair noticed that the hands indicated 3 a.m. and it was at that exact moment that a movement outside caught his attention. Looking through the window, he saw a large, silvery, disc-shaped object hovering about one hundred feet above the grassy space opposite the flat.

He later estimated the 'saucer' to be 60 feet across with round porthole windows on the upper sections. Through the windows shining light was clearly visible. Allistair gained a clear impression that the disc was metallic, possibly because of its silvery sheen. As they looked at it, the object appeared suddenly to hurtle towards them, although Allistair thinks that the disc may, in fact, have been moving all the time and only given the appearance of hovering. It soared above them over the rooftops and rapidly disappeared from view.

The unexpected appearance of the disc left a powerful impact on Allistair and his friends. They felt that it was generating a particularly powerful 'aura', one that could almost be touched and tasted. To Allistair especially it seemed almost 'divine' and he remains convinced that 'it was definitely not from this planet'. The three friends were, he explains, 'dumbfounded' and informed me, in that phrase reminiscent of the '60s, that 'it blew our minds'. Sceptics would probably have laughed at Allistair's comment and remarked that the whole incident was a good example of an overactive imagination. However, in this case, sceptics cannot have it all their own way.

Quite independently of Allistair's encounter and with the witnesses completely unknown to each other, an earlier incident occurred within yards of the same street. In 1955, twenty one years before Allistair's disc shaped sighting, a child had a bizarre encounter in Belhaven Terrace, which abuts onto Westbourne Gardens. The account was given in an issue of *Enigmas*, the newsletter of the UFO group Strange Phenomena Investigations (SPI). Emma Roberts, the pseudonym given to the witness, described the spot where the encounter took place. Today, as at the time, it is wasteland, unused and partly overgrown with trees, shrubs and wild plants. In the summer of 1955 Emma, then eight, was cooking potatoes over a small fire with her sister and a group of older children. Suddenly Emma became aware of strange entities or 'beings' as she describes them. She found she couldn't take her eyes off them. Her sister was frightened by the appearance of these 'visitors' and Emma told her to run home.

Emma, on the other hand, was fascinated by the sight and continued to watch, wondering all the time who or what these people might be. Were they nuns? (There was a convent nearby). Were they engaged in some secret business? But to all these thoughts, even as a child, her mind came back with a clear 'no'. They were something else altogether.

The two entities she had first spotted were now joined by several more. All of them seemed focussed on the ground and completely ignored the children. Emma now realised that they were floating rather than walking and that all these beings looked identical. They were tall, thin, very pale skinned, wearing long, floating, white, plain garments with white caps. Emma was particularly struck by their eyes which were noticeably deep and penetrating, within distinctly pointed faces.

All at once, as if a spell had been broken, one of the entities turned towards Emma, almost as if he had 'tuned in' to her presence. He moved up the slope towards her, looking not at her but through her. All the visitors then turned and followed the first. Emma was now convinced they were not human. She turned and ran. She doesn't tell us, but presumably all her friends took the same action. Anyway, there is no record of the beings chasing anyone all the way to their houses. Whatever they were after, it was clearly not their youthful spectators.

To return to Allistair McNeill, it is interesting that the disc emitted a buzzing and humming noise as it travelled. Allistair emphasised that it was a clear, dry night, with good visibility. The object stood out against the sky with a sharp and clear outline. There could be no mistaking what the three of them saw.

It is probably significant that Allistair is an actor, as it is a profession which attracts sensitive people who are traditionally more psychically aware. That is not to argue that the sighting was a phantom of the mind. The UFO was seen by two other witnesses at an identical moment, suggesting that the disc, whatever it may have been, possessed some form of objective reality.

Another example of UFOs and the artistic mind interacting concerns the case of the Glasgow UFO group CEIV. Indeed, it was the sighting of a 'bright amber saucer' in 1985 which led to the formation of the group. CEIV is short for 'Close Encounters of the Fourth Kind', a UFO research classification indicating contact with extraterrestrials. CEIV used to 'skywatch' (a term used by Ufologists to describe a night survey of the sky for anomalous objects) when they caught sight of a fuzzy, orange shaped, star sized object coming towards them from the north east. The 'saucer' moved noiselessly and clearly did not appear to be an aeroplane of any known type. Some months later, the group were assured by some 'experts' that their sighting was of a smoke ring! An explanation which hardly seems likely, given the length of time of the sighting. Furthermore, the object was followed with binoculars and thus the witnesses found the so-called 'explanation' lacked a little in credibility.

CEIV's UFO was observed from a garden in the higher contours of the city, but some sightings have taken place right in the centre of the historic town. In December 1990, Maria Mortimer was standing at a bus stop outside the branch of British Home Stores situated in the St Enoch's Shopping Centre. Being 4.30 in the afternoon, it was, at that time of year, night, but the skyline stood out sharp and clear. Looking towards a carpark, Maria saw what at first seemed an unusual silver coloured aircraft. Although it was the size of a plane, it appeared round-shaped, with a belt of amber lights across its centre. Maria pointed out the mysterious object to the lady standing beside her, a complete stranger, and together they watched it as it traversed the town centre at roof top height. Gradually, it moved southwards, very smooth in its flight, Maria noted, till it slowly drifted out of her vision. Unusually for such an incident, the sighting lasted for at least five and possibly as long as ten minutes.

Even more astonishing is the fact that this encounter, over the heart of Glasgow's commercial centre, is no isolated happening. In November 1979, just one week before Bob Taylor's Livingston incident, a man walking near George Square, scene of many a political meeting and the famous 1919 riot, watched in amazement as a football sized object sped by him. It emitted a high pitched hissing sound and after this near collision the witness could smell a strong odour of sulphur hanging in the air. Mr McDougall described the object as being spherical in shape and grey in colour. But the fact which struck him as being of most significance was that the sphere moved as if it were operating under some kind of control. There are obvious parallels here with the Bob Taylor incident which was to occur a few days later.

Bright lights were reported by several witnesses hovering over the Maryhill area of Glasgow in July 1988. They stayed in the area for around ten minutes and one of those who watched this display, Mrs Savage, was convinced that there was something mysterious about the invaders and that 'it was definitely a UFO'. In this case the object was viewed at a distance, but Mr Cowan near Cumbernauld not only saw a bright object with a long tail travelling fast, but experienced more direct contact. As the UFO travelled by his window, the whole bedroom was lit up as if by powerful searchlights. This incident is very similar to the Grant incident in West Lothian (recounted in Chapter One), and both occurred in 1992. No source for the sudden brightness other than the mysterious object could be found.

It should be noted, however, that whilst Bob's sighting was clearly of a solid object, Mr McDougalls's UFO has similarities with that object known as ball lightning. This is a round shaped glowing ball of light which sometimes seems to move as if it has intelligence and is aware of its surroundings. Science has yet to offer a convincing explanation of this strange force.

A famous ball lightning case took place in Crail, a picturesque fishing village on the Fife coast. The fiery globe moved across the foreshore, terrifying anyone unlucky enough to find themselves in its path. It seemed to move as if searching for something or someone, wandered into a beach cafe, then eventually disappeared beneath the waves with a hissing sound.

George Square has always been a haven for political radicals, but for UFO sightings too, it seems. A decade after Mr McDougall's encounter a couple crossing the east quarter spotted an octagonal object hovering in the sky above them. Being, they reckoned, about 30 feet across, they felt sure that it would have been visible to all around them. Yet, to their astonishment, everyone else seemed oblivious to its presence. Suddenly, in a brilliant flash of blue, it vanished.

Bright lights, white or coloured, are a feature of Glasgow sightings, as elsewhere. On 9 November 1979, the same day as Bob Taylor's encounter, a lady in the Easterhouse district watched an unusually bright light in the heavens. The light split into two equally bright objects which moved around the sky before reuniting and, as mysteriously as they had arrived, vanished into thin air. The West of Scotland UFO Group have been investigating a mysterious sighting which took place on the evening of 9 October 1994. A British Airways stewardess was driving back to Troon when she caught sight of a strange object. She reported, 'I had just turned towards Lugton when I became aware of a very bright light coming onto the driver's seat. It was this incredible bright light hovering there. The thing must have stayed there for about 10 to 15 seconds ... then it literally shot off into nowhere and it was dark again'. The witness, who had spent twenty two years in the aircraft business, was convinced it could not have been a plane because 'nothing man made could move that fast'. She added, 'I have never seen anything like that in all my years of flying'.

The famous green light phenomenon which has plagued the East coast for years has had its parallel on Scotland's Atlantic coast. At 4.30 p.m. on 27 November 1992 a bright green light was spotted by a witness in the Kingsway area. The object entered a cloud, deliberately, it seemed, then shot away at tremendous speed as if not wishing to be seen.

Occasionally, several lights will appear and seem to form a pattern. In the summer of 1987 Mary McShane from Pollok was standing in her front garden when she saw a group of lights moving in formation high up in the sky. It was 11 p.m. and, as Mary describes it, 'each light was twice as big and bright as the stars which formed a distant backdrop. There were seventeen in total, forming two corresponding arch shapes with an inner and outer arch'. The lights seemed to fade to nothing, then would reappear in exactly the same spot. Was this simply the reflection in the sky of ground based lights? It might be considered as a possible answer, except that Mary was not the sole witness. A few days later the *Daily Record* newspaper received a letter from a man who had seen an object shaped like a shuttlecock in the same area of the city. Distance being difficult to judge, especially at night, it has to be a guess as to whether Mary saw several single objects or one large one. It would surely have to be big to show seventeen separate lights, but at least one witness reported to me catching sight of an object over a mile long hovering over Bellahouston Park! Furthermore, a separate witness during a full moon spotted a 'large space craft' coloured grey, which eventually turned out to be 'as big as Hampden Park' over the Govan area. The same witness has claimed to have seen several UFOs in the area of the sky surrounding the constellation Ursa Major. This association with one part of the heavens is not one which has previously been reported and may result from the particular individual's perception of incidents. Unless there is a case here of 'channelling', which is not claimed by the witness, there seems no reason why there should exist a link between reported UFOs and a star group many millions of light years away.

Incidents investigated by the Lanarkshire UFO Group and compiled by Paul Grey provide further evidence of strange happenings. In 1982 Michael and Carol Stafford were waiting for a 'bus in Bellshill. Carol glanced skywards and caught sight of two bright lights coming towards them. She was struck by the fact that their approach was noiseless, but also by the movements of the lights from side to side as if they were being shaken. Then the object was above their heads beaming a light down on them. Clearly something odd was going on. Michael grabbed hold of Carol and the children, pulling them away from the light and heading in the opposite direction as fast as possible. As they looked back they saw the object, yellow in colour and triangular in shape, shoot off at an amazing speed. Intriguingly, in July 1996 a red, glowing object, shaped halfway between a boomerang and a crescent, was seen moving on a zig-zag path above the area.

Talking of triangular UFOs, from time to time particular types of UFO appear frequently among those reported by witnesses. In recent years the triangular shaped object has been seen over various parts of Scotland, although in my experience it has not established itself as Scotland's typical UFO. I would need a lot of convincing that the 'typical' UFO actually exists. However, there is a widespread belief that the triangle structured craft is one that has become a more common sight in Scotland. It is fair to say that not all reports of this UFO type are anywhere near identical. Typical, perhaps, is a sighting made by Margaret Barrie of

Leonard's Road in Ayr, on Scotland's West Coast.

A former executive secretary, Mrs Barrie considers herself an unlikely UFO witness. She was no skywatcher before her encounter, but afterwards she wrote that the incident had turned her into 'an almost compulsive sky-gazer'. Like so many witnesses, Mrs Barrie felt 'definitely privileged to have seen such a strange sight'. I found her a compelling witness.

On the morning of Friday 6 September 1996 Mrs Barrie stepped into her garden to hang out a family load of washing. It was a good day for drying clothes with the sun shining and a good breeze, and only a small scattering of clouds. Not far from Ayr lies Prestwick Transatlantic Airport. Several flight paths cross the town of Ayr, as I can testify as a former resident. Large, America-bound passenger planes and equally large military craft are frequently seen in the skies overhead. Mrs Barrie watched one travel from the airport in a south westerly direction, probably heading for Dublin. She watched it till it became an invisible speck on the distant skyline.

She was still at the washing line, pegging up a towel, when her eyes were drawn skywards again. She was astounded by what she saw. It was a large, dark object, 'a bit like a delta-wing type plane, but at the same time not at all like a plane as the wings were slowly opening and closing'. She was certain that moments earlier the sky had been clear of any objects, and certainly one as mysterious as this!

The UFO which appeared to be descending slowly stopped at around 300 to 400 feet from the ground. Mrs Barrie judged its height from that of the training planes she was used to seeing in the area. But this was no training plane. It seemed to hover. 'There was no sound whatsoever,' Mrs Barrie wrote in her report. 'The object was silent. It was "soft" black in colour and, strangely, there was no glint from it, as when the sunlight reflects off metal. There was no glass, no obvious contours. There was no "strangeness" to it and no metallic look.'

She watched the UFO for around ten minutes, fascinated by its strange shape and the mysterious manner of its appearance. Then, thinking about a clearer look, Mrs Barrie ran indoors to fetch a pair of binoculars from the upstairs bedroom. At the same time, she called to a workman, a ceramic tiler, who was helping to install a new bathroom suite.

Unfortunately, by the time she returned to the garden the UFO had moved from its last position. It was now much higher in the sky, travelling at close to 90 degrees, that is, almost directly upwards. Mrs Barrie continued to observe it as it travelled through a patch of blue between some clouds, becoming a small dot until it finally disappeared from view. The time was now 11.45 exactly.

There may, of course, have been other witnesses to Mrs Barrie's remarkable sighting, but no one to my knowledge has come forward. However, as most witnesses do not report their sighting, the absence of corroborative reports does not have any significance. My first thought was that if this object could be identified then it was likely that perhaps some form of experimental craft was involved. In fact, that has been a standard explanation of many of the objects with a triangular or near triangular configuration. However, my inquiries with Prestwick Airport (sited close to Ayr and which houses Scotland's main Air Traffic Control Centre) brought a negative response. It was not a new type of aircraft that Mrs Barrie saw that day, or at least not one that the powers-that-be are ready to admit to. This intriguing sighting will clearly be a continuing challenge for some time to come.

It is often asked if these 'visitors' (if that's what they are) wish to do us harm. One native of Glasgow will give a definite 'yes' to that. I have called him Bill, which is not his real name, and altered certain details of his account to ensure his anonymity. Without these safeguards we would not be able to tell 'Bill's' story.

It started back in the '60s when Bill was a mate with the North Sea fishing fleet. On a warm summer's morning in 1969, Bill stood alone on deck watching the sun rise, a brilliant, golden colour, fairy book style. In fact, he began to believe he was dreaming when suddenly he spotted an object which seemed out of place. Too big to be a plane, and above rather than on the water, so obviously not another trawler, it seemed to defy all explanation. Grabbing binoculars, Bill took in the view with one broad sweep. There could be no doubting his first thoughts. There was definitely a disc-shaped object suspended or hovering just above the water line. It looked like the traditional 'flying saucer' portrayed on countless television programmes, although a humped curvature on top and below gave it an unusual oyster-like appearance. Around the middle gleamed a bright red band.

Bill snapped out of his state of near shock and yelled to his shipmates to come and look. As they arrived on the scene the object raced skywards and disappeared. Several, however, agreed that they had caught a glimpse of the disc just as it vanished. The sea was calm and the weather good, so that visibility was excellent, even for the time of year.

According to Bill, the skipper ordered a note to be made in the log. In spite of several attempts we have been unable to obtain the record that would confirm this incident. There is no reason, however, to doubt Bill's account, particularly in view of subsequent events.

That encounter was to form a pivotal episode in his life, although he could not have realised it at the time. Bill is convinced that in some intangible manner the sighting led his life on a downward path. The memory of the event began to take over his mind so that within a short while he could think of nothing else.

Soon after, Bill's marriage began to fail. He was convinced that his obsession with the sighting and its influence over him wreaked havoc with his relationship with his wife. He began to suffer from nightmares where previously he had been a sound sleeper. Even worse, these nightmares began to haunt him during his waking moments, so that no part of the day was free from the persistent image of an enormous spaceship and its occupants.

By now, Bill had left his seafaring days behind and was enjoying 'landlubber' status at a Welsh radio station. Bright and cheerful on the surface, beneath the daily mask he was fretting dreadfully over the way his life was developing. He kept imagining himself imprisoned by aliens inside a craft from another planet. Bizarre secrets were imparted to him, secrets Bill came to believe. The aliens claimed that thousands of their kind were living openly on the Earth. They looked almost identical to humans and melted easily into our culture. Several of these individuals had been assigned to watch over Bill, and should he dare to step out of line, they would exact retribution. Bill was being warned to say not a word about his experiences.

By now the pressure on Bill had reached breaking point and his marriage cracked. Mentally he was shattered. A doctor referred him to a psychiatrist. He was pronounced mentally ill.

A period of recuperation followed. Bill never doubted that the experiences he had gone through were genuine, but for the sake of appearances and to calm his own mind he agreed with the doctors that the strained relations with his partner had warped his imagination.

Put on medication and returned to the world, Bill moved to Glasgow and managed to find a job. He knew full well that he was not mentally as he used to be, but somehow dredged up the resources to cope with life. Problems that would once have seemed minor now took up all his energy to resolve.

Working in a restaurant, friendships developed with his colleagues. Eventually he felt confident enough to confide in one of his workmates the history of his troubled past. The man listened sympathetically and though he made it clear he found it difficult to accept the story at face value, the mere fact of telling it lifted a weight from Bill's shoulders. Having thanked the chef for listening, Bill turned to replace a pile of meats in the fridge when he noticed one of the waiters eyeing him curiously. Bill mentally kicked himself for speaking too openly. He wished he'd made sure no one had been around to listen. He assured himself, however, that the man's furrowed brow had resulted from overhearing such an unlikely life story. Probably has me down as a 'nut', he thought. Gradually, as the day passed, the incident faded from his mind.

It was to return later with a jolt. To Bill what happened can never be put down to coincidence. Yet, true to form, Bill will blame no one for wondering about or questioning his sanity. That night as he returned home two men grabbed him as he entered his flat. 'They looked just ordinary', explained Bill, 'but what they said wasn't ordinary'. They threatened him in blunt language, told him that this time they would only warn him. But that should he open his mouth again..... Bill admits that he didn't know what to make of it all, though the incident scared him badly. He was frightened not simply because he had been threatened.

Even more terrifying was the possibility that he had imagined the whole thing and his mind was going. But deep down he felt sure that it was fact and not fiction.

The next day Bill went to work as usual and was sacked. Expensive meats which he should, and was sure he had, placed in the freezer had been found lying in the store room. As a casual worker, Bill was dispensable. The management clearly felt that a lesson had to be taught and Bill found himself out on the street. He had no doubt who was responsible. Aliens masquerading as humans. To anyone who asks, 'Bill, why should aliens pursue you?', he replies, 'I have no idea. All I know is that they do. They tell me to keep quiet. To say nothing to anyone. Anywhere I try to work they get rid of me. Maybe I've seen something they want me to forget'.

Before Bill's story is dismissed out of hand, the experience of the United States should be considered. Here, there have been many documented cases of individuals claiming to have been abducted by aliens, some in horrifying and distressing circumstances. Bud Hopkins, who has written extensively on this phenomenon, has set up a centre specifically to deal with such cases. Of course, the whole subject is highly controversial. The experiences of individual abductees often only emerge following hypnosis, although sceptics should note that conscious recall does occur. But are these truly genuine memories of events which actually happened? Or have the memories somehow been created by the patient's own imagination? It seems clear that memory creation can take place under hypnosis and thus the extent of the abductee phenomenon - now comprising thousands of individuals - should be viewed with caution. Nonetheless, it is a problem which deserves to be investigated, and Bill's account deserves serious consideration.

Bill is clearly a candidate for the Hopkins Center. Asked about his mental state, Bill replies, 'I know I'm not normal, but that's because of my experience with the aliens. I'm not lying. There *are* aliens on this earth. The government knows it, but is saying nothing'.

Unfortunately, at the time of writing, Bill has disappeared again. I hope, however, that he will surface so that at a time when abductions are being taken seriously Bill's case can be looked at by the experts.

Of course, there are a good number of people who have experienced a UFO encounter at close quarters and suffered no ill effects. Allan Kerr, twelve years old at the time of his sighting, is a good example of this. He can vividly recall the event which took place on a hot sunny August in 1992. It was the twelfth of the month, the start of the grouse season, although Allan was no doubt too young to realise the traditional significance of the day (unlike the poor grouse!). 'The sky was clear', he recalls. 'There were no clouds around'. Out of nowhere a 'huge, silvery, shiny, oval shaped saucer' appeared and hovered over the house. 'I felt all funny inside', explained Allan. 'My breath was taken away'. Allan's schoolfriends did not take his encounter too seriously, even though there is no doubt that Allan witnessed something extraordinary. Scepticism, it seems, starts young. Allan's drawing of the object he saw depicts a typical saucer shape with a clear (glass?) cockpit on the top and two straight lines along the side.

Although almost every witness to a UFO incident is amazed by what they have seen, it is a rare and fortunate person who experiences such encounters time and time again. Individuals who fall into this group are labelled 'repeaters' and there are very few such to be found in Scotland. Paul, a public sector worker from Cumbernauld, is one.

The path that was to broaden into wide and varied experiences started off in a relatively straightforward manner one October morning in 1996. Paul had set off to work as he did each day, driving by car to the outskirts of Cumbernauld. As he turned left from a junction onto the main Glasgow road he caught sight of a strange object hovering low down over a clump of trees just opposite. It was before 6 a.m., so Paul pulled the car to the side of the road to watch the UFO. He described the object as moulded like a ship's keel, although a drawing he made of the incident shows an object that might have been a disc shape viewed from an off centre angle. At each side of the UFO there was a dull, red, glowing light. He found it, and still does, difficult to estimate its size.

This sighting had a profound effect on Paul. He was convinced that if he had managed to catch a glimpse of one UFO, there must be others moving around the area. Paul was determined to view and photograph these as soon as possible. He was not disappointed. From the balcony of his house, offering a good view of the valley below and tree-lined hill beyond, Paul soon became aware of strange balls of light, not only around the sky, but also over the houses and factories within a mile or two of his own family home. Paul emphasises that these UFOs are 'not big ones, but small, silver coloured ones, undetectable unless you are looking for them'. Some of these objects will actually sit on top of buildings, and according to Paul, who has followed them through his binoculars, chase after cars and planes. He has seen them landing in fields and shooting upwards into space from two spots.

In January 1997 events took a new twist when one of the objects, which had been perched on a factory less than a mile way, flew up to the window of his home. Although the object was small, about two feet according to Paul, it was a spectacular sight. He had no feeling that this was intended as something specifically for him. Nor is Paul convinced that they are aware of his presence. He has no sense of having some special contact with an alien presence which makes his claimed experiences all the more remarkable. Although he says, 'There is so much happening', he adds that 'he wouldn't mention it to anyone' as he doesn't want his sanity questioned.

There is no doubt, however, that Paul has experienced some very close encounters. Whilst I am inclined to feel that a number of Paul's alleged UFO sightings have a natural explanation, such as distortions produced by binoculars, I certainly believe that a number of his encounters fall within the typical parameters of an 'unexplained' incident.

In January 1997, while Paul was lying awake in his bedroom in the early hours, he caught sight of a cone shaped object moving in the skies above Cumbernauld. He jumped out of bed and darted downstairs to grab his camera and snap a few quick shots. He clicked the button, but then the camera appeared to jam. Paul immediately assumed that the spool had run out, but when he looked at the dial he saw that it displayed the number 16, indicating that there was space for several more photographs. Paul then reasoned that the camera batteries might be flat. He swapped them for the ones in the TV remote control. But when he stepped onto the balcony to photograph the UFO the camera still refused to work. Although Paul was completely unaware of the David Evans case (see Chapter 6), interference by UFOs against attempts to photograph them seem part and parcel of the phenomenon.

One of the UFOs had by now come right up to the house and hovered just below the gutter. The other shining objects were rotating above the fields directly opposite the housing estate. Paul found himself fascinated by the one that seemed to have attached itself to his house. 'I couldn't take my eyes off it,' he relates. As he watched, a funny feeling came over him. He felt his 'insides go completely'. He felt intense vibrations, but these came from inside his body as if his internal organs were being stirred up. Paul suddenly became aware of how alone and isolated he was and stepped off the balcony back into his living room, closing the glass sliding door behind him.

Hardly had he sat down to recover when his wife shouted to him from the bedroom, 'Are you still up? It's half past five!'

Paul glanced at his watch. Brenda was right. It was way past his bedtime. He hurried upstairs. Two weeks later the chilling thought struck him: where had three hours of his life gone? He had first spotted the UFO at 2.20 a.m. Every action he had taken after that sighting he went through in his mind. It should only have taken minutes, not even half an hour. Yet it was undoubtedly true that a whole three hours had elapsed. It was inexplicable. The implications have not escaped Paul, a tall, thin, intelligent man, but at time of writing he has not yet decided on his next step.

One final curious fact: it was 5.40 a.m. when the experience with the UFO outside his house ended. It was also at 5.40 a.m. when Paul first saw the UFO on his way to work and set off this remarkable train of events.

In discussions of UFO sightings, I'm continually drawn to parallels between Glasgow and Dundee. One might, of course, argue that there are similarities in that both are wealthy cities built on the back of the Industrial Revolution in a way that, for example, Aberdeen and Edinburgh were not. It is interesting that people often think that the "Broons" cartoon strip is based in Glasgow, whereas in fact it is located in Dundee. In terms of UFO sightings, although both have extremely interesting incidents, the volume of reported sightings has been well below what might be expected. Recently, however, Dundee has experienced an increase in reports. In February 1996 three schoolfriends were taking a short cut through Orchard Park, Broughty Ferry. All of a sudden, the early evening night was transformed into day by an intense bright light. Twelve year old Cameron Steuart, Joane Leach and Graham Birnie looked skywards and were startled to see a bun-shaped object with a row of flashing lights around the middle. From the underside of the craft shone the beam of light which had so abruptly driven away the darkness. The school chums watched frozen as the craft hovered above them, then as if at a signal all ran together out of the park and towards the main street. As they looked back from comparative safety, they saw the UFO floating upwards, then fly over their heads and disappear. The young witnesses arrived home in a state of fright at around 7.30 p.m. Drawings made by each of them showed a very similar craft.

A similarly fascinating encounter took place in Dundee on 24 July 1993. David Anthony from Edinburgh was staying with relatives in the Menzieshill housing estate situated in West Dundee. At 10.30 p.m., a time noted from a television programme he was watching, David, sitting in an upstairs bedroom, caught sight of a bright light in the sky. He thought at first it must be a plane heading for the local airport at Dundee, but quickly realised he was watching no ordinary phenomenon. The light was glowing with a strange intensity, appeared to be hovering and was moving south, away from and not towards Dundee. The spherical ball of light was low down, perhaps as low as 100 feet above the ground, but gradually moved at an elevated angle. Mr Anthony could follow the UFO as from his vantage point he could see a distance of about 20 miles or more. Eventually, after he had watched the object for several minutes, it began to lose its blinding white glow and became hazy. Then, suddenly, the single light split into two, then again into two groups of three or four lights, all blazing white.

When Mr Anthony made some inquiries the following day, he discovered that the airport at Dundee had closed at 8.30 p.m., so he could exclude a plane either landing or taking off from there. But what about military craft? The Ministry of Defence turned remarkably coy, refusing to either confirm or deny the presence of planes of the armed services. From Kerry Philpott at 'Secretarial (Air Staff) 2A', he received a standard disclaimer that the MoD only looks at 'reports of unexplained aerial phenomena in order to establish whether what was seen is of defence significance ... In this particular instance we are not aware of any evidence which would indicate that a breach of the UK's air defences has occurred but have noted your report for our records'.

Mr Anthony was not satisfied by their response, which took him no further down the road of solving the mystery of his sighting, and replied to the MoD that he was only trying to find out whether there was any military aircraft actually in the area at the time. The second response was more blunt: 'details of flight paths for aircraft operating out of RAF Leuchars in July 1993 are no longer available. I am afraid therefore that it is not possible to answer your question'.

Those who have had a long term interest in UFOs will know that when Kenneth Arnold experienced his remarkable encounter with a group of mysterious objects in 1947, he compared their movement to saucers skipping across calm water. On a hot, June day in 1995, Pauline Ford was also particularly struck by the way in which the UFOs she witnessed travelled across the sky. Twenty-three year old Pauline had decided to walk to town from her home in Glasgow's Mount Florida. At around 2 p.m. she came to Eglantine Street and, for some reason, looked up. She was stunned to see what she described as 'a very large white object spinning through the sky'. A drawing she later made shows a clear diamond shape. She thinks there may, in fact, have been two of these. An object somewhat similar to this was seen in October 1996 by Alan, a 34 year old civil servant, in the Anderston area. It was like a star with four diamond shaped sections. Alan studied it through binoculars and although with the naked eye it might have given the appearance of an ordinary star, under magnification it became just a shape of light, 'like a hole in the sky ... it was only a couple of kilometers from me at the most'. It struck him as 'an awesome sight - very beautiful'. Alan was not arguing that this was an alien spaceship, but that whatever it was it had a powerful effect on him, a reaction many who have witnessed UFO sightings have experienced.

But can it really be that alien spaceships are visiting Glasgow? After his experience, Tom Coventry, for one, is convinced that they are. His close encounter took place on the morning of 15 December 1983. Tom left for work at about 6.25 a.m., his usual departure time, and followed his habitual route down Menock Road in the King's Park district. It was a crisp, dry morning, weather which boosted Tom's spirits as he had a bus to wait for at a stop with no shelter in which to hide from a sudden downpour. As he stood wrapped in his own thoughts, his attention was caught by a distant object moving in his direction at a low altitude. A quiet, unassuming labourer, Tom took it for an aeroplane moving in a wide arc. He then noticed spurts of flame issuing from the rear and wondered if it was in some kind of trouble, but as it got close it dawned on him that this was not a plane.

All around him things began to go quiet (ufologist Jenny Randles' 'oz' factor), as if he had entered another world. The object had now come right above his head and stood hovering not more than twenty feet away. It was like nothing he had seen before, neither plane, helicopter, nor any other earth-made machine.

'It was coloured grey', reported Tom, 'shaped like a railway carriage, but with a curved roof'. From it there issued crackling and humming sounds as if it was sparking electricity. Being so close, Tom could easily recall afterwards the three porthole shaped windows at the front through which he could make out an interior swirling with yellow smoke.

Slowly the object moved off towards a nearby railway bridge. There it stopped for a second, then shot skywards vertically before heading across the city. Tom watched it disappear in the distance. According to Tom, 'One of the strangest parts was when it did start moving, noise from all around started up again. It was as if it all rushed back!'.

Equally strange, however, to Tom, was the fact that no one else seemed to have witnessed the incident even though a bus arrived while the object was still visible. Passengers on this bus, believed Tom, must have had the chance to see it. Infuriating, too, was the absence of the milkman who Tom always saw at that time on his rounds, except that morning! It was the one time he failed to turn up.

Never a day goes by without Tom thinking of that fateful encounter. Tom openly admits that he was developing at that time a serious illness of which he was unaware. Nonetheless, he is convinced that his health had nothing to do with his remarkable encounter. Nor should it have had. It is clear that encounters of Tom's type happen frequently enough for us to state categorically that UFOs defy a down-to-earth explanation.

Curiously, Tom's flying railway carriage was not the first such object seen. As far back as 1916 an aeroplane on the lookout for enemy zeppelins spotted 'a row of what appeared to be lighted windows which looked something like a railway carriage with the window blinds drawn.' This incident occurred in Essex on a January night, so the pilot's view of the UFO was nothing like as clear as Tom's. Unlike Tom, he was not fascinated by what he saw, but shot at it with his pistol. The UFO immediately vanished.

'Flying saucers' are typicaly imagined as disc or oval shaped, but although 'railway carriages' are unusual, square shaped UFOs are regularly reported. In October 1996, for example, Margaret Dewar of Sauchie near Alloa spotted a strange object like a flying box as she lay on the couch looking out of her sitting room window. It was 3 p.m. and the sky was clear with only scattered cloud. The object was moving slowly and making no noise. Checks with Edinburgh Airport confirmed that no planes were in the area at the time, although the space above the Ochils is regularly used for stacking incoming flights.

Is it pure coincidence that Scotland's earliest reported UFO sighting also involved a witness at a 'bus stop? In July 1947 Andrew Cherry was a 22 year old bottle making operator, employed by Woods Bottle Works in the Portobello district of Edinburgh. It was 5.30 on a beautiful summer's morning, as Mr Cherry waited at his usual 'bus stand close to St John's School in Baileyfield Road. Glancing skywards, he caught sight of a strange object. It was disc shaped with a large, glass dome in the style of an observation window. The UFO was hovering at about 300 feet above the ground, close enough for Mr Cherry to get a clear view of its humanoid occupant. (The 'alien' was wearing dark clothes and was sitting or standing beside a control panel of some kind.) He also noted the marked metal texture of the spacecraft 'like rough diamonds' and the 'orange yellow colour' which may have been, he thinks, simply a reflection of the sun's rays. The area around the object looked hazy, possibly caused by the object's energy source. Mr Cherry could hear a low, smooth hum, which he associated with the flames he could see escaping from the disc. He reckoned it to be 12 to 15 feet in length, but showing tremendous power as it tilted, spun away and disappeared over the Fife coast in a matter of seconds. Mr Cherry describes his experience as 'ghostly, eerie and awesome'. It made such a profound impression that 47 years have not worn it away. As Mr Cherry himself says, 'after all this time I still have chills run through my body'.

Perhaps Glasgow attracts unusual shaped objects, from the Bellahouston gargantua mentioned earlier to Tom Coventry's railway carriage. It's not often, however, that a UFO is to be captured on camera, particularly one with a bizarre shape. But that's what James MacLean managed in December 1995. The object he caught on film near his company's headquarters in Mount Vernon was shaped like a flying dumbbell. Also in the sky at the same time and in close proximity was a long thin shaped object much like a traditional disc shaped UFO. These mysterious objects were caught on film in bright daylight in full view of anyone who happened to be in that part of Glasgow at the time. No one appears, however, to have reported seeing these strange manifestations. This incident does raise a number of important questions. If we are to argue that UFO incidents are somehow psychic phenomena, how can it be that an individual can catch them on a normal camera film? On the other hand, if UFOs have an objective reality, how is it that no one saw the objects at the time? And this incidentally includes the Mr MacLean who snapped the photos. He saw nothing of the UFOs when he took the shots and only realised that he had something extraordinary on film when he had the spool developed. A curious incident occurred at the same time which may or not be coincidence. Mr MacLean himself is unsure. A compass he had in his pocket reversed itself at around the same time that he was photographing (unknown to himself) the UFOs. It is now a perfectly useless piece of equipment.

FIVE

A VERITABLE QUAGM

Any statistical analysis is inevitably fraugh one fundamental issue: what is the source of t is it representative? It would not be possible t following review of UFO incidents in Scot reflection of ufology in Scotland. The lack stretching back into the 1950s makes that a diffic there has not been a Scottish based UFO grou from the '50s to the '90s or any considerable pa could have collated a solid set of data. The res inevitably slants the conclusions towards any period f evidence has been collected.

The best body of cases which has been collected period since 1979. With that proviso, the details discussed random (if there is such a concept) from the database built up by Earth Mysteries Research, plus cases currently being processed. There are at this point details on over 700 incidents (including multi-witness reports). This includes cases personally investigated and details of past encounters passed on by informants, reported in newspapers and magazines etc. It includes only a sample of the 200 to 8,000 (depending on the source) allegedly reported at Bonnybridge, mainly because only about a dozen of these incidents have been reported in detail. A full account giving time, object, etc, is awaited.

Each of the incidents on the database has been analysed under headings relating to witness details, time details, object details, etc. It would be wrong to argue (and I do not attempt to do so) that this gives anything like a full picture of UFO encounters in Scotland, but it is a long overdue first stab at drawing back the curtain on an area previously hidden almost entirely from view.

If we examine, as a first step, the standard number of witnesses involved, it would seem that in Scotland the 'typical' incident is witnessed by a single individual: this accounts for 48% of the cases included in the survey. However, where statistics are concerned nothing is quite what it seems to be. Cases involving two witnesses comprise 16% of the sample and three witness cases make up 8% of the sample. In 17% of cases we know there was more than one witness but are unable to determine the exact number involved. In 16% of reports the number of witnesses is unknown. Presumably, even with new physics, we can assume there was at least one witness! But in the absence of more information it seems sensible to remove this group from the equation. Consequently, we have a situation in which we find that although the largest single group consists of single witness cases, 36% of incidents involve two or more people. Of course, to use the term 'witness' is exclusive. Who is to say that, in fact, there was only one witness to a particular incident? In some cases, for example Bob Taylor's, we can be fairly sure that only one person saw the UFO. In others, particularly unexplained lights in the sky, several witnesses may not have reported it for a variety of reasons. It is probably more accurate to talk of single witness 'reports' and, in so doing, it has to be admitted that such a redefinition takes us a good bit back down the road we just came up.

Bob Taylor's famous encounter is perhaps the best known Scottish single witness incident, but it (and Pat Macleod's Edinburgh sighting) stand up well in comparison with several multi-witness cases where natural phenomena have clearly been misinterpreted. I would, therefore, suggest that having several witnesses does not immediately label a UFO incident as more difficult to explain than a single witness case. In Scotland, we have substantial incidents involving both groups.

Is UFO reporting in Scotland a sex specific occurrence, that is, is it linked predominantly to men or women? Commonsense and the history of UFO incidents in other countries would lead one to believe that sex linkage does not occur. The evidence in Scotland would tend to support this, although men were in a clear majority, reporting in 37% of the incidents where the sex was known compared to 20% who were female. It would seem, therefore, that men are more likely to *report* an incident, although it is necessary to be cautious because in 26% of cases the sex of the individual was not known. In 17% of cases, the witnesses were of both sexes and both (or all) came forward to give their accounts. Overall, the evidence relating witnesses to either sex does not produce startling insights. Both sexes report and are witnesses to UFO incidents, although it appears that men are more likely to report such an encounter than women. It does not show, however, whether men or women are more likely to have a UFO experience.

Turning to geographical location we enter even more uncertain ground. For example, what do we use to define such a concept? We can pick a city, such as Edinburgh or Glasgow, which gives a reasonably recognisable area, but if we say Fife or Perthshire does it make any real sense? And, when you consider it, does relating a UFO to Glasgow or Edinburgh really stand up? What we are talking about in most cases is an airborne phenomenon which may be at any point in the sky, so that a viewer in Edinburgh may be witnessing an object miles away. Essentially what the database has documented is the spot from where the witness saw the incident and thus we may have a general approximation of the area where the incident occurred. I can't give any solid reason for the following geographical division except that it refers to areas which have long been recognised as having an individual identity, cultural or otherwise. The list is in descending order:

Table 1: *Geographical Locations* *(figures rounded up to the nearest half percentage point)*

Mid and West Lothian	42%	Pentland Hills	3%
Edinburgh	13%	Dumfries	3%
Aberdeen/North of Scotland	8.5%	Ayr/West Coast	3%
Fife/Forth	8%	Perth	2.5%
Glasgow	4.5%	East Lothian	2%
Stirling/Alloa	4.5%	Borders	1%
Outer Glasgow Conurbation	4%	Others	2.5%

Clearly the area west and south of Edinburgh and including the city itself stands out. With the addition of the Pentland Hills, the incidents account for 58% of reported incidents. This compares startlingly with the Glasgow area, which accounts for less than 9% of sightings. No other area compares with the Edinburgh area. Fife accounts for 8%, although arguably that might come within the Edinburgh ambit as a number of sightings were reported over the Firth of Forth or along the coastline, certainly within sight of Edinburgh. Further north, Aberdeen and a general area labelled 'The North' accounts for just over 8%, although Orkney and Shetland have been included in this general list and, on their own, account for a proportion of these cases. Some areas of Scotland come in at a surprisingly low level. The Borders, for example, account for 1% only, although the area covered is quite large and though not heavily populated does include some significant centres of population. It is also notoriously plagued by military aircraft on low level manoeuvres, so that a significant proportion of military 'UFOs' would be expected to register. That does not appear to have happened. It is anomalous, too, in that other extensive areas such as Dumfries and the well populated area round Perth also register low down the scale at 3% and 2.5% respectively.

The reason for the predominance of the Edinburgh area seems obscure, but one that I have remarked on on a number of occasions. On a strict population basis, one would expect the Glasgow area with at least double Edinburgh's population to account for the largest number, or, at least, come near to meeting the East Coast's tally. Surely misidentified planes cannot be the answer as both Edinburgh and Glasgow have airports in close prioximity to the city centre with regular military and civil flights crossing over both cities.

A further curious fact is that UFO incidents decrease significantly at Edinburgh's eastern border. East Lothian accounts for only 2% of incidents compared to West and Mid Lothian's 42% and the capital's 13%. Why? True, the airport is located on Edinburgh's west side, so that fact may account for some part of the difference, but the area is frequently flown over by all types of aircraft and people are well used to plane movements. Indeed it is the fact that objects clearly are not planes which leads witnesses to report their sightings.

Admittedly, the limitations of the database, as was noted, must to an extent skew the figures. The focus of a number of UFO groups has been the Edinburgh area, the defunct 'Scottish Research into UFOs' for example. SEMR is based near Stirling. Given the proximity of the Edinburgh area one might expect a greater volume of sightings to come to the attention of active ufologists. On the other hand, SEMR, for example, has made consistent attempts to gather information from the Glasgow area, but even publicity about UFOs does not produce anything like the volume of cases which flow from the Edinburgh area. It is also worth noting that if only a proportion of the alleged 8,000 sightings from the Bonnybridge area were included, the dominance of the area between Edinburgh and Stirling would be utterly overwhelming.

We have a real puzzle here. Even though factors indicated above load the figures towards an Edinburgh predominance, it by no means explains the conundrum.

UFO sightings were reported in Scotland as early as anywhere in the western world following the Arnold incident. The earliest encounters we have recorded, however, date from 1947 in Edinburgh and 1952 in Glasgow. From 1947 to 1996 there have been regular reports of incidents, although the period 1974 to 1976 registers a noticeable dip, whereas 1979, the year of Bob Taylor's famous encounter, produces a notable peak. The biggest incidence of cases recorded occurred in the years 1990 to 1992, particularly 1991/92. There has been an annual rise in reported incidents from 1986 to 1990 (excluding 1987), but with a dramatic increase in 1991 and 1992, then a sharp decline in 1993. The years 1993 to 1995 show a remarkably consistent flow of reports. If we look at the proportion of reports by decade we find the following:

Table 2: *Reports by Decade* *(figures rounded up to the nearest percentage point)*

1990s	71%	1960s	2%
1980s	18%	1950s	1%
1970s	12%		

Obviously, the 1990s stand out. In fact, the period 1991 to 1992 alone accounts for 55% or over one half of cases recorded.

Clearly, of all the figures these must be the least reliable and underscore the problem of any UFO investigator working from a limited database. The data collected represents periods when UFO groups were increasingly active in Scotland, from the mid 1980s onwards. The 1991/92 peak in part represents the phenomenal response to the UFO hot line set up by SEMR and SRUFO, which produced a flood of reports relating not only to the year 1992, but for the whole period from 1950 onwards, although the greatest number were for relatively recent cases.

The truth is that we won't have a clearer view of UFO incidents in Scotland over the last 40 years until considerably more cases are brought together on a single database and analysed. This, of course, is also true for all the aspects of UFO data that has been surveyed in these pages, but especially so if we wish to assess annual fluctuations in UFO reports which, I would suggest, is a key problem in this whole mystery.

Accepting that months are arbitrary divisions of time, nonetheless it is interesting to note the fluctuations in the levels of UFO reports from month to month. In terms of the information available, we're on firmer ground here. Again, however, we are looking at a broad sweep based on overall figures rather than an annual cycle. The incidence of monthly reports produces the following table:

Table 3: *Monthly Incidence* (figures rounded up to the nearest half percentage point)

Month	Overall % of Reports	Month	Overall % of Reports
January	6%	July	2%
February	2.5%	August	15%
March	7%	September	9%
April	4%	October	18%
May	3%	November	23%
June	6%	December	8.5%

The October to November period immediately stands out although the reasons for this peak don't immediately seem to cry out. Sceptics might point to the onset of 5th November with its displays of fireworks brightening the night skies. Superficially, this might seem an attractive solution, but the argument would only hold if the types of UFO reported were different from objects seen at other times of the year. Or if November's UFOs had something in common which set them apart from UFOs seen throughout the year. In fact, November sightings are much the same as incidents witnessed in spring or summer, equally intriguing whatever the season.

Furthermore, there is no evidence that after 5th November there is a steep decline in UFO reports. In fact, what we see is a rise from September (9%) which reaches a peak in November (23%) and then falls back through December into January which comes in at 6%, halfway up the league of twelve.

Mystics, of course, might point to the October/November peak and its association with the pre-Christian Celtic calendar. October 31st is Hallowe'en and the start of the old Celtic year (Samhain) is on 1 November.

The proportion of reports from February to May remains at a steady level, between 2.5% and 3.5%, although March at 7% bucks the trend. Thereafter there is a rise to 6% in June, but the year's low point comes in July with 2% of the total. The latter may be due to the fact that July is the traditional holiday month in Scotland, schools having broken up at the end of June. Perhaps there are simply fewer people around to report? On the other hand, with time to spare you might think that there would be more attention paid to unusual lights in the sky. The Press at this time of year is particularly desperate for stories. Whatever the reason, July comes bottom of the league of monthly UFO sightings.

Thereafter, there is a sharp rise in reports to August which provides 15% of the annual total. Despite this upward surge, it is noticeable that even including February's lowly 2.5% most sightings occur during the months of early darkness, that is, October to February, which account overall for 58% of the total. Before jumping to conclusions, we should also bear in mind that 42% of sightings take place in the lighter months and if long hours of either darkness or light affect the number of reports, why does February account for only 2.5% and June a not staggering 6%? The position may be a little clearer when figures relating sightings to hours of the day are considered (see below). In broad summary, the evidence seems to point to there being more UFO reports in the latter part of the year than in the earlier months. There is no clear explanation for this. Furthermore, these figures do not relate to an annual or even a ten yearly cycle. It cannot be claimed that the numbers that have been used represent a standard which has been constant. It is perfectly possible that the monthly incidence of reporting has altered over a period of time and analysis of past decades might produce a different picture. There is not enough data to provide a definite conclusion, but at least I hope I have brought the runners to the starting block.

In terms of time of day reported, UFO sightings generally happen in the evening. A remarkable 42% of incidents take place between 9 at night and 1 in the morning. It is a safe bet that after that most potential witnesses are fast asleep, and the lowest incidence of reports is recorded between 2 a.m. and 3 a.m. Afterwards, while there are some variations, the rest of the day moves within the range of 2% to 5% apart from a flurry of activity between 8 a.m. and 9 a.m., the commuter hour.

The late evening to early morning bulge might explain why the darker nights predominate. Less light makes objects harder to identify, produces more lights in the sky and leads to more reports. Interestingly, the types of UFOs seen appear to be split almost evenly between objects classified as unidentified lights and those where a solid object is reported. The appearance of humanoids represents only a fraction of incidents, around 4%. Contact with alleged aliens in Scotland happens in only a handful of cases. It may be that with increased publicity over alleged abductions there will be a corresponding rise in Scottish reports. It will be a good barometer of the reality of the UFO phenomenon to document its development over the next few years in Scotland.

How do UFO statistics north of the border compare with elsewhere? No comparison has been carried out in the sense of an agreed range of questions set against a comparable database drawn from, say, England or the United States. Such an exercise would be a fascinating one to follow through. In the book *Fact or Fantasy* Jenny Randles does report an analysis of UFO incidents carried out for the United Kingdom (which presumably included Scottish cases) for the period 1975 to 1979. It is an engrossing account and it is interesting to compare that sample with our Scottish one to see what, if anything, is similar and what is different. Does this comparison shed any light on UFOs? As might be guessed, the highest proportion of cases involved unidentified lights in the sky (about 87%). This is probably a slightly lower proportion than might be the case in our survey, but is in general line with it, that is, the single largest aspect of the UFO phenomenon involves a reporting of mysterious lights.

In terms of the number of UFO witnesses, the survey reported by Jenny Randles gives only the *average* number of witnesses, which comes to 2.19. I'm not sure that this statistic can tell us a lot about the nature of sightings, as it is obviously an amalgamation of witness figures which might vary significantly. Still, it does point to the fact that witnesses to a UFO incident are on the lower side and doesn't seem too out of tune with the Scottish survey.

On the sex of the witnesses, there does seem to be a significant difference. Sixty eight per cent of the non-contact UFO cases were male and the figure for UFO contact cases was similarly high. This compares with 37% of male witnesses in Scottish cases (17% of males involved two witness cases). The difference seems difficult to explain, even if we assume that by the 1990s women were more inclined to report a UFO encounter than in the '70s (which is a big assumption). It may be that the data simply does not have the accuracy or the sheer bulk to provide a useful comparison. It does, however, point to the broad conclusion that men are more likely than women to report a UFO incident.

On the issue of which time one is most likely to see a UFO (which is then reported), the UK survey named 9 p.m. The Scottish survey noted that 42% of reported sightings take place between 9 p.m. and 1 a.m., although it did not purport to identify one particular point in time. Statistics are a well known quagmire, particularly to the non-specialist, so it would be wrong to come to any definite conclusions. Arguably, the UK and Scottish surveys do point broadly in the same direction, if not along the same road. It would be interesting to compare sightings from different periods from various areas within the UK and see if any comparable trends are evident. If there is one sensible conclusion, it is that a lot more research needs to be done before we can draw a firm picture of the nature of UFO sightings in Scotland and the UK.

SIX

FROM UFO BASES TO BONNYBRIDGE

Plagued as Scotland has been for decades by UFO sightings, one question haunts the minds of investigators. Where do these mysterious objects go when they disappear from a witness's view? Find the answer to that conundrum and you will probably have solved the whole UFO phenomenon. Some UFO buffs have argued that there must exist a dimension parallel with our own which may or may not be aware of our existence, but somehow interacts with us. UFO visits are, consequently, either intended as a deliberate investigation or an accidental intrusion into our earth's airspace.

Other explanations are no less mind stretching. Authors have claimed that there are UFO bases located deep beneath the seas or hidden inside the interior of the earth itself. This last speculation has even coined a name, 'The Hollow Earth Theory', and in this strange world of mirrors has gained a considerable following among the more extreme ufologists. Compared to these solutions to the UFO enigma, the belief that these objects may be spaceships from a distant planet, capable, by far, of exceeding the speed of light, appears almost straightforward and levelheaded.

But would UFOs, even if they truly are alien spacecraft, regularly use an area of Scotland as a base to land and take off? There is one man who is convinced through his own observation that they do. He is David Evans, an active 70 year old, living near the small city of Dunblane a few miles from Stirling, the ancient capital of Scotland. From a hill directly behind his home, Mr Evans has gazed in wonder at the antics of, not one or two, but dozens of 'flying saucers', as he unashamedly labels them.

Mr Evans's story is an extraordinary one, even in the annals of ufology, which is itself a history of the bizarre, but is in keeping with the exploits of a man who came to Scotland with the army during World War II. When the allies triumphed he stayed on in Caledonia, serving out his years as an employee of a public utility. His retirement has certainly not meant a period of quiet contemplation. UFOs have seen to that.

Aware that there are many only too willing to laugh off his claims, David has made a great effort to obtain evidence to back up what he has witnessed in the surrounding hills. He has snapped dozens of photographs of the alleged landing site, several of which, he claims, show UFOs and capture on film the methods used by the 'saucers' to defend themselves.

David Evans continually shows willingness to exhibit to anyone with sufficient interest to travel to his house his collection of UFO snaps. He is always ready to discuss his claims. He will even take you to the alleged landing site if you are fit enough to stand a walk of several hours over rough and boggy terrain.

David's experience started during 1992 when he was involved in a close encounter with a spaceship. The alien craft travelled from the hill overlooking his patio garden, towards and above the village rooftops, then disappeared from view behind the high ground beyond. Because it passed so close, Mr Evans had a good sighting of the object. He was struck by the grid shaped 'mesh' that seemed to form a protective skin enveloping the vessel. It was metallic, or appeared so, glistening in the sun as it sailed over David's head, clearly under the control of some form of intelligence.

David Evans, being the character he is, was not one to let the matter stop there nor to run to the press with a sensational story. Instead, he determined to carry out his own investigation to see if he could find out where this UFO had come from. He was to be staggered by the facts that emerged.

Perched on the summit of the hill overlooking his home, David kept a watch on the mountains which rise and surround the village where he lives. One particular peak soon attracted special attention. It was a ben situated about ten miles away, but one that through the binoculars David usually carried could be brought almost within spitting distance because of the clear Highland air. Evans watched and waited, certain that sooner rather than later an object would reveal itself and confirm what his instincts told him.

It was, however, an incident much closer to home which convinced him that he was without doubt onto something extraordinary. One night in his sitting room he became aware of a strange glowing light. It seemed to be penetrating far into the kitchen from the paved backyard. David knew immediately - though he is not sure why - that the object responsible for this interruption was not of this earth.

Gingerly, he made his way past the armchairs into the kitchen and, standing well back, looked through the double-glazed door into the yard. The glass was opaque and so David could not make out clearly the source of the mysterious light. Its intense beam, however, he could quite plainly discern. As he had sensed, but hardly dared to believe, there was 'something' out there, fairly small yet solid and emitting a powerful pulsating light.

Cautious enough not to open the door for a closer look, David had a brainwave and crept into the bathroom from which a window overlooked where the UFO stood. He flicked on the light then headed back for the kitchen hoping that he might now get a clearer view of his visitor. His bold move didn't pay off. The object, perhaps sensing that David had become aware of its presence, had in that short space of time disappeared. This unexpected visitation had, however, been long enough to convince David that in his surveillance activities he was on the right track. The watchers knew they were being watched.

Tactics adopted by the UFOs, if they were deliberate, didn't worry David. They intrigued him. Even when a UFO entered his house he wasn't put off his pursuit. Although he didn't see the object on this occasion - 'they were too smart for me this time', was his verdict - the UFO left telltale signs which David was quick to latch onto.

He had left the window of his front room open and so, in the garden, heard a strange humming sound come from the interior of his bungalow. When he looked inside, he discovered a round depression formed in the carpet with the pile distinctly pressed down. It seemed as if a small yet heavy object had recently rested there.

Perhaps, he reasoned, the object had not actually made contact with the carpet, but moved on a cushion of pressurised air. The force might be strong enough to make a permanent impression on a soft covering. Whatever the explanation, there was no doubt in his mind that the mark had been produced in some extraordinary way. David knew, living on his own, that he had not been responsible for it. And if not him, then the likely perpetrator boggled the imagination. An object, he felt sure, of extraterrestrial origin. Its visit to his house had not been an accident. The point that bothered him was whether it was intended to 'warn him off' or a friendly indication that he was on the right track and must continue his investigation. Later incidents would not resolve this issue which even today after so much has happened remains obscure.

From then on, David made frequent and increasingly determined efforts to photograph the 'flying saucers'. He succeeded, he believed, on a number of occasions. The photos, however, revealed an even more tantalising glimpse of our alien visitors, according to David. The UFOs deliberately 'spiked' his photos so that the pictures of the mysterious objects he had caught on film were blotted out by a peculiarly shaped and multi-coloured form. From one end sprout pink fingers of flame, as if the UFO had rushed by just as David's finger pressed the shutter.

To David, the fact that his pictures were deliberately obscured was further proof that he was dealing with an intelligence of some kind. The objects, he argued, had been sent by a controlling 'mother' ship. As in the Bob Taylor case (see Chapter One), they were remote controlled devices sent out to protect the UFO from prying eyes.

Whilst no one can doubt David's sincerity on the matter, it has to be said that others have offered straightforward explanations to account for the photos David has taken. To at least one professional photographer, the prints show only an 'alien' spot or reflection caught by the lens. Mr Evans vehemently refutes such a mundane solution to his unidentified object and points out that it appears on the negatives neither before nor after the ones on which it is seen. David argues that the UFOs have the ability to merge into the background, and can adapt their form to that of the surrounding area. That explains why it is difficult to spot a UFO which may be sitting on a hillside because it can camouflage itself to a degree unimaginable to our intelligence. A report from a UFO incident which occurred in July 1975 near Machynlleth, Powys, shows that Mr Evans' explanation for a UFO's invisibility may not be so far fetched. According to the witness to the 1975 sighting 'the light atop the object and inside the base began to glow and pulsate in a strange mixture of colours that exactly matched the scenery ... it simply went into the background like a chameleon camouflaging itself ... after a few moments it was not there anymore!'

If there truly are alien craft using this remote glen as a base, would they be aggressive and even be prepared to destroy one of our terrestrial aircraft? David Evans shows no doubt on the matter. One May morning *The Scotsman* newspaper reported: 'The crash of an RAF Hercules near Blair Atholl, in which all nine on board were killed, was caused by a low altitude stall, an accident report said last night'. But Mr Evans had a completely different view of the matter.

On the afternoon of the disaster he had been out walking in the hills near the town of Comrie. An ex-army man of wartime vintage, he claims familiarity with aircraft sounds.

'A big one went over', he later told me, 'I could tell by the noise it was making. I knew it wasn't a jet'.

As the sound of the propellers receded, David watched as one of the disc shaped objects, by now well know to him, passed above the hill-tops. Late that evening David learned of the Hercules crash and guessed its cause. The UFO, suspecting that the plane had been sent to monitor its activities, had downed it to warn off further interference.

That night, David rang me and informed me of his experiences. Initially, I was sceptical. It seemed too incredible a story to be true, and more out of a 1950s science fiction comic, one of the pulp kind. However, given such a mind bending story, it was necessary to do it justice and, consequently, I did enquire at Glasgow Airport, who referred me to Prestwick, about plane movements in the area. I was told that there weren't any that couldn't be properly accounted for. Whatever David had seen, it could not have been another aeroplane.

Through investigations carried out, it emerged that the Hercules, of which there were three travelling together, had followed separate routes although, of course, they were heading in the same direction. One of the routes did seem near enough to Comrie for David to have heard the noise of its engines. I was startled by this revelation. It seemed that here was independent confirmation that David could possibly have heard the Hercules passing at the location and at the time he claims. A hill walker caught David's attention as the plane roared on, although he naturally did not think of taking the man's name. If he were to come forward now, it would provide additional evidence in support of David's strange encounter.

There is one other possibility. The NATO air base at Machrihanish used to be one of the biggest in Europe with a runway reputed to measure over one mile in length. For several years rumours have multiplied over the nature of the secret activities that were carried out at this site and the experimental craft that may have landed here. Most people will have heard of the top secret Area 51, a vast protected area in the United States. It is a key military installation where it is claimed devices including alien spacecraft are kept and tested. Was Machrihanish Scotland's Area 51? There is no argument that it would be the first choice airfield in Scotland from which to operate aircraft technology the government wanted to keep secret. That would include devices allegedly developed from captured alien discs. Or, so the conspiracy theorists argue, even brought to fruition with the help of extraterrestrials, with whom our generals have supposedly made contact! Far fetched, certainly, so let's keep our feet firmly on the ground. It is definitely possible, even probable, that the latest in aviation technology has been brought to Machrihanish. It is equally likely that some UFO reports have occurred because of sightings of these advanced machines. But would they have led to the crash of a slow moving Hercules? Did an accident occur which was hushed up because of the involvement of secret, state-of-the-art aircraft? David Evans would no doubt disagree. He firmly believes that he has seen alien machines. But, given our government's notorious secrecy, no explanation can be ruled out.

About 50 miles to the east, and north of the Forth Estuary, Ian Macpherson, a 45 year old resident of Rosyth, also believes that he has photographed a 'flying saucer'. 'Is it a hub-cap, a hoax or a UFO (Unidentified Fife Object)?' ran the less-than-serious *Daily Record* headline of 28 February 1994. Ian himself, however, appears perfectly straight-faced about his encounter and upset by the manner in which the tabloids have treated his snaps of the UFO.

Ian tells a credible story about his encounter. While walking one February Saturday round Craigluscar Reservoir near the town of Dunfermline, he heard a peculiar humming sound. It was 3.15 p.m. Glancing skywards, he caught sight of a strange object. According to the *Dunfermline Free Press* the object moved around for about 15 minutes and came quite close to Ian, but Ian only thought to grab a couple of quick shots as it moved away.

'The craft's acceleration was phenomenal,' reported Ian. 'By the time I wound the film on it was a dot in the sky'. He estimated its size at around 60 feet. The paper quoted him as saying, 'I was holding my camera, but felt unable to use it. I have never experienced such feelings before'.

Ian generously handed over the photos to the *Daily Record*, which was sufficiently impressed to print them for its readers and also forward a set to the Ministry of Defence.

UFO investigator Malcolm Robinson commented, 'It is the most exciting photograph I have ever seen in this country. These pictures are really remarkable. I have never seen anything like them in this country before.'

It was stated that Ian watched the 'craft' for around fifteen minutes, although in conversation with me he has said that it was difficult to be clear about the time involved. He described the UFO as 'definitely metallic' with 'several points of diffused light on its underside inside a darker coloured rim'. The points of light do not appear evident in the photograph. However, Ian drew a sketch of the craft before the photos were developed. The sketch and photographs are similar although, probably as they were viewed from different angles, not identical. The upper section of the UFO as drawn in Ian's sketch appears larger in proportion to the remainder than in the photo. The underside and prominent grill-like flange are not seen in the shot though clear in the sketch, which shows the lower portion of the UFO tilted away from the viewer, whereas only the upper section is visible in Ian's snap.

Oddly, the *Daily Record* published a blown up and rather fuzzy version of the UFO. The local paper, the *Dunfermline Free Press*, published in contrast a very clear picture which included background against which the UFO had been seen, that is the reservoir and surrounding trees. As the *Daily Record* version appeared before the *Free Press* publication I was thrown by the clarity of the latter and what it depicted. The snap in the Fife paper seemed remarkably like a clay pigeon used in target practice and competitions: a similarity which had been masked by the *Record*'s close up and consequently less clear image.

UFO investigator Ken Higgins visited Craigluscar reservoir soon after Ian's picture appeared. The background in the picture certainly matched that at the reservoir. Ian had definitely snapped the UFO at the spot he said he had. Ken noted that the area was one used for clay pigeon shooting. It was littered with broken and unbroken clay pigeons. Ian, however, appears perfectly sincere in his story and readers will have to be the judge of the matter. The balance may be in Ian's favour, particularly as Nick Pope has stated that the Ministry of Defence were unable to identify the object.

Certainly, Fife has had its share of UFO reports. In May 1996 bar stewardess Margaret Mellon saw a mysterious object pass over Saline Hill. It was around 3 a.m. when Margaret was woken by her sister-in-law Janet Duffy who drew her attention to a bright orange light tinged with blue which seemed to illuminate the whole of the distant peak. Suddenly, a massive craft appeared and sailed slowly towards them before disappearing over the rooftop of their house. Margaret's view of UFOs was dramatically transformed by the incident. Before, she had been sceptical of the whole phenomenon, but her own sighting convinced her that something strange was taking place in the skies of Fife.

Local investigator Sharon Coull has unearthed at lease a dozen previously unknown incidents in the 'Kingdom' (as Fife is often referred to in Scotland, because of its historic independence). One, for example, dates to 1988. Sharon reports that 'a woman living at Simon Crescent, Methil, was cooking one night when she saw a bright light in the fields at the back. There was also a loud noise which made her think that a harvester was at work. She got concerned when the noise got closer and the kitchen went bright. As she opened the back door to investigate, there was an object in her back garden which then shot straight upwards and out of sight. The woman's parents who were in bed also heard the noise and their room was also lit up'.

This incident has echoes of several other cases covered in this book. What on earth is going on? Why do the authorities turn a blind eye to these incidents? Sharon Coull was also closely involved in investigating the alleged alien sightings covered later in this chapter.

Why should an extraterrestrial spaceship visit a Scottish gaol? I can think of no good reason and yet the puzzle over what we are dealing with is laid bare by the sighting of a UFO at Glenochil Prison. The incident occurred during the night of 15 May 1994 when a brightly lit object was spotted hovering around the perimeter fence surrounding the complex. This wasn't the chance glimpse of a human witness. The prison surveillance cameras had caught the object as it scanned the huge mesh fence - escape-proof according to the authorities. The UFO was then seen to move backwards and forwards above it. The prison officer who witnessed the object explained, 'It was a bright white light with a big hole in the middle, like a giant polo mint'. A curious fact is that two officers sent out to investigate what was going on claimed that they could see nothing. Yet back in the control room the white light was still plainly visible on the video screen. The spokesman for the Scottish Prison Service responded to enquiries by stating that the 'logical explanation' was 'camera fault'. Reasonable, if the only evidence was the view of the UFO via the surveillance equipment, but evidence has come to me that other prison officers did see the object with their own eyes, which might explain why the original video footage disappeared. Videoed over, it was claimed, in order not to waste tape, although I don't feel that the saving of public money was justified in this case! It must be asked, why was the tape re-used if it was considered faulty? If the surveillance camera was not working properly, why was it not reported? There is no evidence that any action was taken to repair or replace the allegedly faulty instruments.

Overall, the lands north of the Forth have seen their fair share of UFO incidents. In 1986, the town of Alloa, for example, witnessed a bright circular shaped object circulating in the night sky. It was the peak summer month of June and so even though it was 9.30 at night the witnesses had a clear view in the brilliant sky. The UFO was never identified.

On the same day a few miles west in the village of Menstrie a blue circular object was observed for ten minutes hovering (perhaps watching?) high in the sky. It was a similar object which appeared six years later to a witness in Sauchie, a community to the north of Alloa. Travelling along the A907 which connects both towns a driver saw a bright hovering light. He stopped the car for a better view and noted that the UFO made no noise as it moved. It travelled slowly, drifting towards a farm, then suddenly vanished as if a cosmic finger had switched a light off. This was presumably the same object which appeared over the nearby village of Fishcross on 22 July 1986. A blue circular light was seen by a male witness. It hovered over the area for a few seconds, again as if watching, before moving off.

In 1989 Alloa resident Graham Sharp spotted a multi-coloured diamond shaped object moving over the former mining village of Cowie lying on the south side of the Firth of Forth. It was an April night at around 10 p.m. when Graham and his wife Shelley caught sight of the UFO. The object appeared to be slow moving and they were able to follow its manoeuvres for almost half an hour as it changed colour from red to yellow, then green and blue.

'At first I thought it was a planet', admitted Graham, 'but it was definitely moving'.

As a former soldier and familiar with aeroplane silhouettes, he knew it could not be a conventional craft. He was so convinced that he was seeing something out of the ordinary that he called out his neighbours to take a look.

They were sure that the object required further investigation. However, when the police arrived they could see nothing unusual! Inspector Alec Brown was reported as saying, 'We had Air Traffic Control check the area and they reported that nothing was flying over Cowie and they saw nothing untoward.' The policemen made the sensible explanation that huge lights on the cardboard factory in the area coupled with weather conditions caused the light to appear to be moving, and confused the witnesses. Graham, while conceding that the factory illumination sounded a plausible cause of his sighting, was adamant that the lights were moving. If that was the case, then the Sharps certainly saw a UFO.

In March 1997 the police were again called out to investigate a reported UFO. The witness, Gillian McNeill, was out walking her dog on the sloping ground above Lornshill Academy on the outskirts of Alloa. It was an early morning exercise Ms McNeill carried out dutifully every day of the week. On this morning, however, her black labrador stopped suddenly and 'started whining with fear', she recalled. She noted the time as 5.25 a.m. The dog simply refused to go any further. Wondering what could be causing the problem, Gillian spotted a strong beam of light shining through a row of trees directly ahead of her. It seemed to be pulsating 'on a regular rhythm' and at the same time changed colour 'from pale cream through to yellow spectrum to deep yellow and back to cream again'. Ms McNeill estimated that the light spanned a width of about 30 feet. Clearly, a large object must have been the source of the glow.

Baffled and concerned, Gillian, after watching the light for about ten minutes, decided to call the police and walked over to a nearby phone box. As she dialled she glanced at the UFO where 'the light stayed constant, neither changing shape nor size'. The policeman who took her call sounded sceptical, but agreed to send over a couple of men who arrived shortly after. Ms McNeill had suggested meeting at the back of the Academy so they could get the best view of the strange light.

However, by the time they met up the pulsating light had disappeared and all that could be seen was a pin-point of light to the right of the original. 'If we're not back in five minutes, call the polis!', joked one of the officers as they headed up the slope, watched anxiously by Gillian. She saw them reach the spot where the light source had been situated and then walk about waving their torches in every direction. After a few minutes they gave up the search and returned down the slope. It was at this point that Ms McNeill noticed a very strange occurrence. At the spot at the top of the slope where the police had been standing seconds before were two odd figures, walking methodically backwards and forwards. Ms McNeill describes what happened next, 'When the policemen came back beside me, they said it had only been a burning log, but that they would arrange for the firemen to come and check the log later in the morning. As they spoke the two figures were still clearly visible at the edge of the trees. I said to the policemen, "If you are back here, who are the two figures up there?" and I pointed to where the policemen had been'. The two young officers seemed taken aback by this and quickly departed, stating that they would have to write up their report!

It's perhaps significant that Ms McNeill's labrador would not go near the trees on Friday, but by Saturday willingly went up to them. Whatever had frightened her had now clearly left the area. Gillian is adamant that 'whatever caused the light was not a burning log, nor a reflection from a street light'. If that is the case, what did she see? Two entities from another dimension? And why did the police miss these 'people' when they were so close to them? It is a puzzle to which we are still seeking the answer.

An alleged UFO, however, seen over the naval base of Rosyth was tracked down. Several witnesses on an Edinburgh bound Loganair flight spotted a fast moving diamond shaped object in the night sky. It certainly struck those who observed it as something out of the ordinary. Research by Ken Higgins revealed just how careful we should be of even the most honest witness and the most dramatic looking event. He discovered that the UFO was actually a group of phantom jets from nearby Leuchars RAF base flying in formation. Although it turned out to be an IFO (Identified Flying Object) it should act as encouragement for serious investigators. It shows that it is possible to explain what looks at first sight to be inexplicable, and thus adds strength to those cases where the identification of a UFO is not possible even after the most meticulous investigation.

Rosyth lies on the north shore of the Firth of Forth. On the opposite bank lies South Queensferry, the departure point, before the road bridge was opened in 1964, of travellers to the Kingdom of Fife. Unlike the Rosyth sightings, however, several incidents from the south side of the Forth are still unexplained. Perhaps the strangest emerges from a photograph allegedly showing a strange blurred object beside the yacht *Lady Barbara* snapped at the same moment as a distinct splash was heard as if a large object had entered the water. The estuary was calm at that time and there appeared to be no natural explanation for what was seen and heard.

Such events are food and drink to those who argue that UFOs are not extraterrestrial in origin. There are those who suggest that these alien visitors are less 'alien' than we think and have their homes underground or underwater, where prying terrestrial eyes find it impossible to locate them. Deep water sites in the Pacific are obvious areas where detection would be difficult. It is surprising then to learn that such bone crushing depths are not necessarily favoured by UFOs. In Puerto Rico, for example, bizarre shaped objects can be seen emerging from shallow water within easy sight of land. The Forth would provide a comparatively safer hiding place. It would also provide a solution both to the many sightings in the Forth area and why UFOs seen there appear to disappear so suddenly without trace.

And yet ... it has to be asked that with the volume of sea traffic ploughing the Forth, wouldn't *someone* have seen *something* definite? Of course, a lot of the lane movement is military, and you wouldn't expect anything to be revealed in these cases. Others might have seen incidents so incredible they would be afraid that no one would believe them. And who could blame them? Some have argued that, in any case, the 'visitors' can cloak themselves in some form of invisibility so that they can operate very close to our shores and escape detection, all the while spying on our military installations. But that, surely, would be stretching credulity to the limit.

Any object seen on 5 November 1992 naturally raises the question, 'Was it a firework?' Particularly when the UFO in question appeared as a green light. The witness, however, is adamant that the object she saw had no connection with Guy Fawkes celebrations. On the contrary, it is the very fact that it contrasted sharply with coloured explosions that so obviously were a part of the festivities which attracted her attention. The object moved high in the sky at, she guessed, around 500 feet and, though it was the green glow which caught the eye, the witness got the clear impression that it was somehow solid. Perhaps she meant that the light originated from a solid object which was also using a beam as a means of concealment.

On 2 February 1992 a woman in South Queensferry was woken by a bright flashing light. Gingerly, she opened her curtains and saw what she could only describe as 'a big block flying'. Although it was 12.50 a.m., she immediately phoned the police. Interestingly, the flashing light could be explained by the local coastguard searching for a suspected suicide. The Forth Road Bridge and Railway Bridge are well known launching points for those seeking a quick end to their problems. However, neither the police nor the coastguards could explain the large object witnessed by the terrified woman.

The blue light seen by witnesses in the Alloa/Clackmannan area may have returned in 1992. A witness noted a bright blue object travelling between Kincardine and Grangemouth. The UFO appeared to be moving at speed and headed in an easterly direction. On this occasion, no solid object could be connected with the light. However, a solid object *was* seen on two separate occasions in 1992. A witness in Kinghorn on 24 November 1992 spotted a strange low flying UFO which did not look like any conventional aeroplane. As it moved, it did so silently. Was it a secret government aircraft? A few months previously, in August, a family saw a brightly coloured object moving southwards. The UFO was the traditional circular or disc shape. In the same month and in the same area a man saw a bright beam of light descending to the earth and soon after a bright object could be seen moving slowly north.

A more elaborately shaped object was seen by a witness in September 1992. A young girl observed something she described as being similar to 'a long Christmas decoration'. From her account the UFO clearly had a flange running around the outside. The object was sufficiently out of the ordinary to interest RAF Leuchars. It clearly was not a sighting of one of their planes which led to the report and they, in their turn, forwarded an account of the incident to the Ministry of Defence in Whitehall. So far the mysterious UFO has not been identified.

Of course, no discussion of UFO cases in Scotland's central belt would be complete without a reference to Bonnybridge, labelled the 'UFO capital of Scotland' (like Blairgowrie before it) and allegedly the heart of a UFO 'triangle'. A triangle which, it is suggested, covers an area of intense UFO activity stretching from Fife to the borders of Stirling on the west and reaching to the fringes of Edinburgh on the east. There is certainly an element of truth in this designation in that West Lothian, for example, has experienced repeated incidents out of all proportion to its size and population density.

If Bonnybridge (population 5,500) does indeed have, according to local councillor Billy Buchanan, over 2,000 witnesses to UFO sightings then it truly is a world hot spot. A similar proportion of witnesses to population would in Edinburgh give about 200,000 witnesses. Truly a lifetime activity for any UFO researcher!

Events in the area started quietly enough with a number of interesting although typical UFO reports. These incidents took place as early as January 1992 when during that month a Mr James Walker witnessed a cross shaped formation of stars hovering above the road as he was driving along. He stopped his car and looked back, noting that the lights had now assumed a triangle shape. Mr Walker was understandably mystified by the incident which he felt could not be put down to any obvious source, such as an aeroplane. However, perhaps the best known incident took place in March of that year. At around 7 p.m. the Slogett family were walking towards Bonnybridge when Steven Slogett caught sight of a circle of light. He drew the attention of the rest of the company to the strange phenomenon. The light appeared to land in a nearby field. The family walked on, but were halted in their tracks by a football sized blue light hovering or resting on the road ahead. Isabella Slogett later reported, 'My daughter Carole and I saw a UFO land right in front of us. A door opened and there was a howl-like sound. I screamed and ran off terrified'. According to Carole, 'There was a flash of light as if we were being photographed'. When they reached their home at Leonard Drive, Bonnybridge, the mysterious object was still visible and, it was said, was seen by several other witnesses.

According to the February/March 1993 edition of *Enigmas*, the newsletter of Strange Phemonena Investigations, the Slogett family had a second encounter with an object which flashed its lights at them, although Malcolm Robinson expressed the view that this 'could well have been a car or large vehicle containing a courting couple'.

Reports continued throughout 1992 with a Mr Anderson reporting a 'bluish white light, very bright, which disappeared behind clouds', and a father and daughter joint witnesses to a triangular shaped object, both these incidents occuring in November.

Another interesting report occurred in 1993 when Ray and Cathy Proceck, driving to Cumbernauld to visit friends, spotted 'an elliptical shape with bright lights around the edge'. As they passed beneath a viaduct they opened the sun roof of their car to get a better look. When they reached the other side they were rewarded by witnessing 'an identical craft'. Both objects were triangular shaped and completely silent. Before the incident neither Ray nor Cathy were interested in UFOs, but were convinced that they had seen something they could not explain.

It was not the nature of the incidents, however, which attracted media interest in the area, but rather the sheer volume of sightings which were relayed to the media by local councillor, Mr Billy Buchanan. He explained that his constituents were coming forward with reports of UFO encounters and that it was his duty, therefore, to seek an explanation of the incidents. No solution, however, was forthcoming, in spite of the efforts of UFO investigator Malcolm Robinson.

By the end of December 1992 over 200 witnesses to events were being cited by Billy Buchanan and a public 'skywatch' announced and broadcast via the television network. Naturally, as a result, considerable public attention resulted, although to the disappointment of those who turned up, including the TV cameras, ET declined to appear. The attention, of course, generated more reports of UFO sightings and some ufologists began to question whether it was now possible to disentangle the origins of the reports from the sightings inevitably generated by media interest. It is well known that individual reports of UFO incidents increase when existing incidents are highlighted: what previously was simply a light in the sky becomes a UFO because an atmosphere of 'UFOism' has been created.

In order to calm the situation, a public meeting was arranged at the Norwood Hotel in Bonnybridge by Billy Buchanan for Sunday 31 January

1993 at 7 p.m. The *Sunday Post* newspaper reported that, 'A town plagued by UFOs has called in the experts as concern grows among residents'. Councillor Buchanan was amongst those claiming to have seen a UFO and added, 'I've had around 400 calls in the past few months'. The article revealed that some of the town's residents would 'be hypnotised in a bid to find any subconscious memories of being taken aboard an alien spacecraft'. In the event the hypnotist did not turn up although nearly 300 did to hear Malcolm Robinson lecture on world wide UFO incidents, including alleged abduction cases.

At this point Scottish Earth Mysteries Research in a radio broadcast urged caution over the Bonnybridge sightings until a proper investigation had been carried out and the number and nature of the sightings could be accurately assessed. As events moved rapidly along it was clear, however, that media interest was not going to be side-tracked by the concerns of any UFO investigators!

The arrival of a Japanese film crew provided the opportunity for some interesting speculation on the Bonnybridge sightings. In the *Stirling Observer* Malcolm Robinson was quoted as being 'convinced that Bonnybridge is one of the world's few "windows" to another dimension'. Meanwhile, according to the reporter, Councillor Buchanan had more than UFOs on his mind. The story ran, 'Councillor Buchanan seemed to have a well thought out game plan ... He said he hoped the crew would have relatives back in Japan who could pull some weight'. 'Hopefully,' announced the Councillor, 'one of the crew will have an uncle called Mitzubishi who might want to build a factory in Bonnybridge'. The report continued, 'Councillor Buchanan denied that it had been his intention from the start ... "Why shouldn't Bonnybridge benefit? We have a superb setting here and Central Region is a friendly and inviting place"'. The article concluded with the revelation that 'Councillor Buchanan has a special surprise in store for the Japanese group - a massive cake shaped like a flying saucer'. The Japanese were suitably impressed by this display of Bonnybridgean hospitality. However, attempts to secure financial backing for a 'giant glass mushroom shaped visitor centre', intended as a UFO tourist attraction, failed to get off the ground, according to *The Daily*

Record.

Meanwhile, as Bonnybridge was claiming the title of a 'world hotspot' for UFOs, the same description was being applied to Edinburgh, a mere twenty miles down the road. Were the UFOs seen in Bonnybridge identical to what was being witnessed in the Lothians? Disappointingly, as Scottish ufologists argued about the nature of the Bonnybridge sightings, the potential for a comparison, for piecing together the jigsaw, was overlooked.

Meetings arranged in Falkirk, whilst attracting huge attention and raising the profile of ufology in Scotland, did not really move the investigation on and by encouraging people to consider every odd light in the sky a 'UFO' may have muddied the waters rather than cleared them.

Some aspects degenerated into farce, as writer Edward Talisman irreverently described in *Phenomenal News*, over a supposed alien called 'Zal-us'. Mr Talisman wrote: 'Sceptics of the Bonnybridge "hotspot" were given added fuel by the unfortunate antics involving "Zal-us" and the "Council of Nine". Zal-us, according to some newspaper reports, was an alien who had an important message to give to the world. The message was going to be revealed at a meeting in Falkirk Town Hall, one evening in October. The hall had been booked for the affair, by Councillor Billy Buchanan, no less. So Councillor Billy was at the centre of this enigma? The tabloids seemed to think so and one, (the *Daily Star*, I think) labelled the unfortunate Buchanan "Bonnybridge's Crackpot Councillor". Indeed, to be fair to the press, someone, somewhere, seemed to have put words into Billy's mouth which appear to suggest that he had personally met an ET who claimed membership of some galactic body which was overseeing the development of the earth (obvious, isn't it?). All in all, it made a great read, and, caught up in the excitement, I was devastated to learn that it had all been a load of ..... nonsense. Billy Buchanan had never met an alien, and the name Zal-us was alien (all right, completely unknown) to him. Mr Buchanan was, it transpires, utterly blameless and bemused and justifiably annoyed at his name being taken in vain. So where did Zal-us come from? Without revealing all the twists and turns of a murky plot, it seems that another UFO group had somehow picked up the name. But where from, I don't know. Anyway, according to *The Scotsman* the name originated with Ufologist Malcolm Robinson in his newsletter. However, claims Malcolm: "I don't know how the name Zal-us crept into the article ... I would never put in some false data ... just to jazz it up!" An enigma indeed!'

Meanwhile, genuinely odd incidents were taking place in the area. In October 1994 three cleaners working at the Union Chemical Factory at Carronshore saw five UFOs as they were on their way to work. Beatrice Campbell reported that she had first noticed the UFOs at around 5.40 a.m. She described one large object which had a light orange glow and four smaller ones sparking on and off. The larger object appeared to be sending out beams of light to the smaller sparkling objects. Beatrice reported her sighting to their manager Bill Downie. Soon other employees were coming forward to give their accounts which seemed to indicate that strange objects had been appearing in the area for some days. Diane Keating from Camelon had witnessed the previous Wednesday at 7 p.m. a reddish shaped ball which disappeared and then reappeared. She was sure it could not have been a plane because she saw one fly under it. At the same time Steve Lewisham saw a 'bright white' object which moved in a direction away from them, then 'came back and began to glow red and orange. It was going really fast. We saw a passenger plane with its landing lights on underneath it. The object was very much faster than the plane.'

One fascinating aspect of the UFO sightings in this area is the extent to which UFOs have been caught on video. According to the *Falkirk Herald* one was even captured on police video cameras! The cameras turned to film an object reported by Catherine Penman of Hallglen, near Falkirk. Her husband, Scott Penman, first spotted the UFO at around 10 p.m. According to Catherine, 'It was a really bright light which was down quite low. At first, I thought it was a star, but it was ten times bigger than a star and was really close to the house. There is no way it could have been a helicopter or a plane because of the length of time it hovered in the air. I contacted the police because it was so unusual.'

Even greater publicity was given to film footage caught by sixty-three year old Margaret Ross of Stenhousemuir. Her video of an object seen in May 1996 shows a bright light criss-crossed by stripes of different colours.

Margaret and her husband Alex (72) spotted the UFO as they were preparing for bed. It appeared to them disc-shaped and brighter than a star, and struck both witnesses as being of really strange appearance. As they videoed, the UFO appeared to zoom toward the house. There is certainly no doubting the unsettling nature of the couple's experience, although some UFO investigators believe that the camera may have unintentionally doctored the image of a natural object.

However, in October of the same year Margaret Ross was again fortunate to catch another UFO on video. At first the white object which she was videoing to the south of her house pulsated for about 15 minutes. Then it gradually changed, transforming into a half moon shape with intensely bright bars travelling diagonally across and a glowing outer shell. Mrs Ross caught sight of the UFO after she got out of bed at around 6 a.m. In a strange twist, her daughter Alison, had also spotted the same object from her front room window a couple of miles distant. She watched it for some time before ringing her mother at 7 a.m. to draw it to her attention. Mrs Ross, of course, had already been videoing the UFO for an hour, but was delighted to have independent confirmation of what she had caught on film.

Some of the best video evidence may be found on film taken by the Malcolm family of Larbert. This shows an object taken during daylight hours which even the Ministry of Defence has been unable to identify!

It was stories such as this which led to people from all over the UK to visit the area, some with the intention of establishing inter-galactic contact. One such group from London, MASSER, commented that 'the aliens like to keep us guessing right up to the last minute'.

Events in the Bonnybridge area have certainly kept us in suspense. If Nick Pope, the Ministry of Defence executive officer turned ufologist, is correct, there have been over 8,000 witnesses to UFO sightings in this area. A truly staggering figure. Councillor Billy Buchanan, who played such a key role in bringing the attention of UFO experts to the events in his town, claimed a figure of 2,000 witnesses. It may be that Mr Pope with his insider's knowledge of the UFO situation is aware of a large group of reports which has not yet reached the public domain. It is very much to be hoped that in the not too distant future the full extent of UFO sightings in the Bonnybridge/Falkirk/ Larbert area will be revealed and fresh light thrown on a genuine Scottish mystery.

In October 1996 more remarkable video footage was taken, this time by Hallglen resident Barry Macdonald. Barry was driving along Windsor Road in the Camelon district of Falkirk when he and his girlfriend Jane Adamson spotted a mysterious object hovering in the sky. It was around 6.40 p.m. They stopped the car and got out to get a clearer look. After they had watched the object for several minutes, Barry remembered that he had his video on the back seat. Barry is a keen angler and to prove the size of his catch he makes sure he has the evidence on tape. This time he was going to use it to even greater effect. He managed only 30 seconds of film before the object disappeared. But what he managed to get caused a worldwide sensation, featured on many TV programmes across five continents! The UFO appears as an orange oval which changes shape to a white disc. In fact the classic 'flying saucer'. It seems to glow again, then turn white once more before disappearing in the blink of an eye. Whether it simply 'vanishes' or moves away at an incredibly fast speed is impossible to tell. It is there one second and gone the next. Checks with local airports indicated that no known craft were in the vicinity at the time.

It's an accurate saying that 'familiarity breeds contempt'. How often have I heard it said, 'why would so many UFOs visit Bonnybridge', or West Lothian, or other sites which have no particular claim to fame? But does it matter where UFOs are seen? Why choose any one place to another? So it came as no surprise when another alleged close encounter case occurred in Fife. After all, as far back as 1976 an incident involving Christine and a possible abduction scenario had occurred. However, what was different in this instance was that there were many more UFO investigators active in Scotland by the autumn of 1996. Not only Malcolm Robinson, but Gary Wood, David Colman and Sharron Coull were involved. As a result, details of the incident which occurred close to Kennoway near Leven were quickly brought to public attention.

The remarkable series of events didn't start in any dramatic way, but developed from a simple car trip by two friends, Lyn and Jean and ten year old Peter, to a local shop to buy a jar of coffee. It was around 7.30 p.m. (timed by the start of a television programme) on 23 September, dark at this time of year, although by way of compensation it was a clear and dry night.

In an opening scenario reminiscent of the famous Barney Hill case, Lyn, who wasn't driving, spotted a bright oval shaped light low down in the sky. She watched for a few seconds, wondering what it could be, then turned away. When she glanced back, the single light had become two circles the shape of well rounded car lights. Lyn was now intrigued, as the object did not appear to be moving and so, she was sure, couldn't be a plane and seemed too big to be a helicopter.

Lyn drew Jean's attention to the light and both agreed that it was difficult to account for it. A 'UFO', although neither described it as such at this point. Jean, who was driving, slowed the car to a walking pace so that they could get a clearer view. The object was now to their left and seemed to be hovering behind a farmhouse whose silhouette was visible against the gentle glow. Beams of light were seen travelling from the sky to the ground (or perhaps in the other direction. Generally, if there is a light beam, witnesses tend to automatically assume that it is directed downwards. Could it be that the UFO was being guided in?). Suddenly, the field below the UFO lit up like a firework display and illumination burst through a clump of trees that grew alongside, turning night into day all around them.

The explosion of light ended as dramatically as it had begun. The object, which had remained stationary for so long, now started to move and as it did so Jean and Lyn noticed its triangular shape and that it sported a dome atop its uppermost section. The UFO disappeared at a fast pace, rotating slowly to display small red dots of light.

Understandably bemused, Jean and Lyn nonetheless started the car and continued to the local shop. Jean bought the coffee and they set off on the return journey. But on the way back they were again confronted by the strange object as they passed the site of their original encounter at around 8.20 p.m. They first spotted red lights ahead travelling at speed. Then the object turned and headed directly towards them. It lit up a whole battery of lights for an instant, then switched them off. And as suddenly as it had arrived, it disappeared into the night. Lyn noticed that three cars were travelling behind them, although there was no indication that they had seen the mysterious object.

Having returned home, the witnesses decided after further discussion to revisit the area of the incident. They were both nervous and intrigued, anxious to resolve an incident which had produced very strange reactions to their minds and emotions. At 9.45 p.m. they drove back and as they approached the site their attention was caught by a blue glow which was visible just above the trees. A star shaped object could also be seen pulsating and emitting coloured streaks of light. These were alternately red, blue and green and thrown out in rapid sequence. Lyn described them as being like torch beams, narrow at the base and widening as they reached upwards. Obviously some inexplicable events were taking place, but no one could have been prepared for what happened next. It would have numbed the senses of anyone and surely shake the narrow outlook of even the most hardened sceptic.

Moving among the trees were several skinny, small entities, definitely not human. Above them in physical stature towered a tall individual, estimated at around seven feet, who seemed to be in charge of his smaller companions. Understandably frightened and perturbed, Jean and Lyn turned the car round and drove home.

Frightened, yes, but, according to the witnesses, still intrigued by what they had seen. Curious enough to decide to return and have another look. This time they had got hold of binoculars, lent by Lyn's brother James. The blue light was still glowing as they arrived, but with the binoculars it was possible to get a much better look. They could see a shimmering ball which appeared to be emitting heat and energy of some kind. It looked amber in colour, with an irregular surface and dark patches. One of these darker patches situated near the base could be identified as an opening. The craft didn't seen to be lying on the earth, but hovering or possibly resting on thin supports. It appeared to be rotating and tilting rhythmically.

To the right of the object, but definitely on the ground, lay a circular disc, coloured dark red but possibly reflecting the amber colour of the ball shaped craft. All around was the proverbial hive of activity. Groups of the small creatures were transporting boxes and tube shaped objects from the wood towards the craft. Lyn described these beings as having 'very big, dark eyes and with heads too big for their bodies. They didn't appear to have mouths'. The taller 'supervisor' was still visible and, say the witnesses, they could make out his brown skin and oriental eyes. The incident had a terrifying ending, described by Jean, 'suddenly dozens of bubble-like things came out of the woods and flew across the field towards us. Then they were all around us, about four feet away. They never moved. They were all alike. We could see through them and each one had one of these small creatures inside. They had big black eyes and big heads. They seemed to have smooth bodies and strange deceiving mouths!'

Later, weeks after the incident was over, Lyn began to have dreams about being taken into the craft. Were details of an abduction experience emerging? The witnesses, quite correctly, were wary of undergoing hypnosis. Their conscious recall of events is the very best type of evidence as it allows investigators to examine the evidence without the worry of 'false memory syndrome', which is thought to occur with hypnosis.

After the incident, strange events were alleged to have taken place which have little, if any, parallel in documented UFO cases. Peter, for example, the ten year old who was present at the original incident, claimed (as reported in the *Daily Star*) that a shiny grey alien was in his bedroom and went down to the breakfast table with him. One alien also accompanied him to school in a taxi and shared it on the way back. As researcher Malcolm Robinson said, 'because information can sound fantastic, does that mean there is no truth in it?' Children do make strange claims about invisible friends and the reality of these particular events depends, in my view, not on the later accounts by young Peter, but on the initial incidents themselves.

Cases such as that in Fife are a real challenge to our belief systems. This is no doubt why the scientific and other establishments are quick to sweep them under the carpet in the hope that they will be rapidly forgotten.

SEVEN

INTERRUPTED JOURNEYS

The United States is undoubtedly the home of the abductee. From New Hampshire to California there are thousands of individuals claiming memories of forcible contact with aliens. So many have now come forward with their stories that a centre for abductees has been set up by American ufologist Bud Hopkins where people can exchange accounts and in this way come to terms with their experience. Mr Hopkins claims to have personally dealt with 500 individuals who have had such experiences. This case load on its own is more than the total reported incidents in the United Kingdom. Where abductions are concerned the US is out on its own.

Who can doubt though that the rest of the world will soon follow this intriguing route as, in so many things, America sets the pace we all eventually follow, albeit in a form modified to our own particular environments. It does seem that the abduction scenario is culture influenced. How else can we explain the intensity of the abduction experience in the States compared to, for example, Great Britain? Or are we prepared to accept the argument that Americans are inherently more interesting to alien intelligence than the average European? Can any sensible person be persuaded that alien contact is a reality and not a kind of modern myth, a re-awakening of the ancient tales of contact with fairies and similar alleged mythological entities? If the whole saga seems less than credible, then, I would suggest, that does no justice to the individuals who have, in all honesty, strange tales to relate. There is little doubt in my mind that inexplicable incidents have affected the lives of a number of people. Incidents for which these witnesses to the bizarre still seek an explanation. Their experiences cannot, must not, be dismissed out of hand, as sceptics in America and Britain would dearly love to do. There is certainly a case to be answered.

First, however, a note of caution.

It may surprise UFO investigators recently arrived on the scene that Scotland was the alleged scene of a very early alien contact case. In 1954, hard on the heels of George Adamski's meetings with Venusians in America, Cedric Allingham drove to Scotland for a holiday. He had picked February for his annual break so Mr Allingham was either ignorant of the climate beside the North Sea or was a hardy type who could ignore the cold. He had chosen the area around Lossiemouth, a well know fishing centre, for a spot of hiking and bird watching.

On 18 February while taking a walk on the coastal path from Lossie to the nearby village of Buckie, Mr Allingham caught sight of a saucer shaped object. It moved away but returned a short while later, at which point Mr Allingham took some photographs. He had by this time realised that here was a truly mysterious craft. His thoughts were confirmed as the door of the spaceship (which had now landed) slid open and a humanoid alien stepped out. Cedric Allingham was able to communicate with the Martian using signs and gestures. After learning several amazing and previously unknown facts about the red planet, Mr Allingham reluctantly wished his visitor goodbye as the space traveller indicated it was time for him to leave. As the disc became a dot in the sky, Mr Allingham wondered who on earth would believe his story. Fortunately, the whole incident had, it turned out, been witnessed by a local fisherman, James Duncan, who testified to the truth of the events. With this sworn statement Cedric Allingham published a book *Flying Saucers From Mars* which caused a sensation. Here was documented evidence with photographs of contact with peoples from another world. Or so it seemed for a while.

Unfortunately for the credibility of ufology in Scotland, the whole series of events were later exposed as a huge hoax. However, it took over a dozen years for the truth to emerge and at the time of the event its accuracy was widely accepted. People wanted to and were ready to believe Cedric Allingham. The revelation that it was fictitious adversely affected the public's attitude towards Scottish close encounter cases. It was not until 1979, twenty five years after the Allingham affair, that the media in Scotland paid serious attention to incidents involving alien contact.

Since 1954, however, encounters with entities have taken a more sinister turn. We talk of 'abductions' rather than 'encounters'. The idea of 'abduction' implies being taken against one's will, rather than the friendly face-to-face chat that Cedric Allingham took part in. This change in attitude as well as the cultural context have affected our perception of what alien contact involves. I would suggest that these variable factors should encourage us to be cautious about abduction reports. There are many disturbing stories, but in assessing such incidents we must try always to locate the wood rather than be spellbound by the trees. We must try hard to be careful and control our enthusiasm, because abduction incidents are at the heart of the UFO mystery and should be objectively assessed.

Bob Taylor's encounter has been discussed already in depth. Arguably, although he was unconscious for a period of approximately twenty minutes, this does not count as missing time. On the other hand, there was clearly a time gap between Bob's physical contact with mine-like objects and his 'coming to'. Bob, to my knowledge, has never indicated that he remembers anything of what happened during this period. It remains to this day a complete blank. Bob, however, has experienced no bad dreams, no frightening afterthoughts and no wakening in the middle of the night in a sweat. He remains what he always was: the calm Scotsman with his feet firmly on the ground.

One fact that, perhaps, separates Bob's experience from most abduction cases is that Bob was out of consciousness for a comparatively short time and has always been clear about the sequence of incidents as they happened to him. Nevertheless, there is no getting away from the fact that Bob for at least a twenty minute period was unaware of anything that was going on around him. We can only speculate given the dearth of other evidence as to what happened to him during that period. Probably he did, in fact, simply lie unconscious on the ground till the barking of his dog brought him back into this world. Whatever the truth, Bob has never shown any signs of worrying about the missing period. Unlike Christine.

Details of Christine's remarkable encounter which took place in 1973 did not emerge till the 1990s when she confided the incident to a friend, Brian. He himself had witnessed a UFO in the 1960s and was soon convinced by the account Christine gave that she had experienced something unusual. He wrote to leading ufologist Jenny Randles who passed the letter to Scottish Earth Mysteries Research as an organisation on hand to investigate the incident.

Clearly, after 20 years there were going to be problems establishing what had actually taken place, but it represented a challenge which we would not have wished to refuse. Intrigued though we became the more we absorbed the broad details of Brian's letter, we did not realise at this early stage just how remarkable and frustrating the investigation of Christine's experience was going to prove to be.

At our first meeting with Christine in her comfortable first floor flat not far from Dunfermline with Brian present, it soon became clear that her strange experience of those many years ago still haunted her.

I have visited the spot of her encounter and, in spite of the passage of time, and the impressive scenery, a dark cloud can still descend on your mind as you picture the events of that evening. Christine, with her friend Margaret, had visited Lochore Country Park one warm August day. They had been taken there by Margaret's parents in a car even though neither family lived far from the spot where they were picnicking. Going by car saved time and youthful legs. The evening passed quickly till, shortly before 9 p.m. when it was still light, they packed up and headed for home. Following a metalled lane out of the park they came to a junction where the green ended and a housing estate began. It was now right on nine o'clock, or so the radio announcer informed them. A car drew up quietly behind them.

All at once, two things happened simultaneously. The radio went dead and the car engine cut out. As if influenced by a magnet, Christine, in the back seat with her young friend, looked to the left across several yards of open ground. Heading towards them strode two veritable giants moving in a rather mechanical motion like machines rather than living beings. Both wore one piece silver suits, emphasising their over-large heads. Christine cannot be sure how long it took the entities to cover the space that separated them, but she does keep a vivid memory of the strange beings getting closer and closer to the car, but the car simply refusing to start. And then the two beings were almost up to the window, within yards of where Christine sat frozen, unable to move. She now experienced a choking sensation and, it seems, passed out at this point. What happened next remains a mystery.

When Christine came to, she saw the backs of the two 'giants' as they returned in the direction they had come from. Moments after they had disappeared from view, a cone of light spread around the trees edging the field, as if marking the path of an object heading skywards. At this exact second the car engine roared into life, to be joined immediately by the sound of a radio. A human voice completed the trio. The driver of the vehicle behind rushed up and shouted, 'What the bloody hell was that?!' Christine doesn't remember if anyone gave an answer. All she recalls is sitting in silence as they continued their interrupted journey.

When Christine walked in the door, her mother's first words were, 'Where have you been?' Her mother reminded her sharply that it was after 11 o'clock. She should have been in long before. Margaret's mother explained apologetically that they 'had been held back'.

After the shock of the parental rebuke had worn off, it dawned on Christine that a ten minute drive had taken nigh on two hours. Or, to be more precise, there were two hours missing out of Christine's life, for neither then nor since has she been able to account for this lost time. Indeed, we are asked to believe that not one but at least five people suffered a time loss: the four occupants of the car in which Christine travelled and the man at the wheel of the car behind. Unlikely? Christine is very convincing on the matter.

The day after the incident Christine mentioned it to her friend's mother, naturally curious and looking for reassurance as most of us would. Christine has told me that the lady point blank refused to talk about the event, telling her in clear language to forget it. It is hard for a 12 year old to be persistent when faced with a wall of adult silence and so Christine did not forget, but said nothing, for nearly twenty years.

It was silence, however, tinged by deep thought and wondering. Christine wanted to find the answer to a problem which nagged and ate away at her. What had happened during those lost hours? Could hypnosis uncover the solution? She was willing to try anything and so a first session was arranged with an authority on the subject who, for professional reasons, does not wish to be named.

The hypnosis session proved dramatic. Christine turned out to be an excellent subject and was gradually and carefully taken back to the very day and second of the encounter. Up to that point Christine had been very calm and relaxed, but as her mind relived the memory of the car engine cutting a dramatic change took place. Christine became visibly distressed and started choking, putting her hands to her throat and apparently unable to speak. Immediately the hypnotist took action to calm Christine and, sensibly, informed us that he thought it better not to carry on with the session because of Christine's severe reaction. I agreed completely. I didn't think that anything useful could be gained and that Christine's distress had been enough to prove that she had been through a traumatic incident at the time she claimed. Clearly, the event had put Christine through an experience she could not remember easily.

In spite of what had seemed an upsetting few moments to those who had watched, Christine emerged in a remarkably calm frame of mind. She suffered not a single disturbed night and even said that she was willing to continue with the hypnosis sessions. She remains determined to get to the bottom of what happened to her.

Hypnosis does not appeal to everyone and has so far been resisted by Andrew Swan. He too has experienced 'missing time' although he, unlike Christine, believes that there is a simple explanation. Andrew's experience began late one night on 30 July 1994. A violent electrical storm had broken up the night sky, and, in order to get a better look at the lightning strikes, he drove to a clear point beside the playing fields at Armadale Academy, a secondary school a few minutes journey time away. Parking his Audi coupé beside the football pitch Andy, a cable layer with Scottish Power, caught sight of a large object hovering behind a row of trees a few hundred yards opposite. He noted that the UFO was pyramid shaped and saw the time by his watch was 11.45 p.m. Andy later commented, 'I thought it was going to crash'.

But the object made no attempt to move and hung motionless as if suspended on a thread in mid air. Puzzled, but intrigued, Andy jumped back into the driver's seat and followed the road which took him to a viewpoint on the far side of the mysterious visitor. As he cruised along the route, however, either the UFO he had been watching or a second object flew low down at head height almost seeming to scrape the roof of his car. The UFO stopped abruptly as did Andy's car with the brake pedal punching the floor. Standing at the road-side, Andy could clearly make out the UFO, shaped like an inverted pyramid, floating either just above or in front of a bing. He estimated the object as being nearly 40 feet long.

The stand-off between the UFO and Andy continued for about 20 minutes, till Andy decided he would, literally, shed some more light on the problem. He chose a simple method which would allow him to get a better view without having to get any closer to an unknown danger. In his vehicle lay a powerful halogen spotlight and Andy reckoned that this could be put to good use without causing an unforseen reaction. Unfortunately for Andy, events didn't work out quite as he had planned.

As soon as the beam hit the UFO, the halogen bulb exploded. Andy took it as a definite signal that the object did not wish to be seen. As he stared at the 'dead' spotlight, the exposed situation that he found himself in dawned on him. He was in the middle of nowhere with not another person in sight. It was high time he left the scene of his encounter. Unfortunately for Andy's emotional state, when he turned the ignition the car refused to start.

Andy had already had the presence of mind to call the police, but had been frustrated by the delay in their arrival and had taken it on himself to shine his torch towards the UFO with the result described. Locked in an immobilised car, his nerves were stretched to breaking point. Then, as he renewed his efforts to get under way, the enigmatic object, like the proverbial 'bat out of hell', shot into the air and travelled over him at breathtaking speed.

Andy grabbed his mobile and dialled the police a second time. As it turned out a patrol car was already on its way in response to the first call, but had been delayed by taking the wrong road. Andy had hardly finished his second call when the blue flashing light came into view.

Andy quickly explained what had happened and was breathalysed at his own request (with a negative result). He certainly had not been drinking that night. On the other hand, the object that had taunted Andy's imagination had gone and so the police were left with a mystery and a car that wouldn't start. The last problem was far easier solved, so the AA were called out to get Andy back on the road. I was fortunate enough to be able to locate the man who answered that call, a Mr Donald Macandrew. According to his records, Mr Swan's call was logged at 2.42 a.m. and the AA were informed that the police were in attendance. By the time thirty-four year old Mr Macandrew arrived on the scene, forty-five minutes had elapsed and he noted the time as 3.36. These timings were to assume a deep significance in due course. For the time being the AA man took note of the fact that his 'customer' gave every appearance of having suffered a real fright. To Donald, Andrew explained how he had arrived at his present situation. Mr Macandrew was struck by the fact that his client repeatedly stated that he had been watching the UFO 'for forty minutes' although, if the times given were correct, three and a half hours had gone by since the mysterious object had been first seen.

Pondering the anomaly, Donald Macandrew tried to get the car started, but it refused to respond to his experienced touch. He turned the ignition and flicked the side lights. Nothing. He poked the fuse box. It looked good. No fuses blown. But the car was definitely dead. It was clear that the only way the car would be getting home was at the end of a tow rope. Then, job done, as he pulled into gear to take his charge away a remarkable event occurred. Andrew's side-lights, previously as dead as a dodo, sprang into life. Thinking a miracle had occurred, Donald turned the car engine over, but the machine obstinately refused to move. As a baffled Mr Macandrew told me when I interviewed him, 'The side lights coming on doesn't make technical sense!'. The following Monday Donald returned to Andrew Swan's house in Armadale, partly intrigued and partly as the conscientious officer who wanted to see if the 'dead' car could be made to rise from the grave again. His astonishment was still obvious some months after the incident when he told me that the car had started as normal later that very Sunday morning of the incident. Andrew had decided to give it a try and, like magic, the motor sprang into life. Both he and Donald expressed themselves baffled by the car's unexpected response.

In fact, in this strange case, there are not one but two mysteries to clear up. What influence was it that led the car engine to stop, then start again wholly on its own? How do we account for the missing time in Andrew Swan's life? He insists that he made a phone call to the police before midnight. But no phone call was logged by the police computer till 2 a.m. What on earth happened during that fateful gap? Andrew Swan claims that there is nothing to explain. The police, he adamantly repeats, must have made a mistake. Officers, however, equally vehemently deny there has been any mix-up, asserting that their version of the timings is undeniably correct. Intriguingly, Mr Swan refuses to undergo hypnosis as he has no wish to discover that even stranger incidents may have taken place during his encounter. That is, of course, whether you would accept evidence obtained in such a session.

A case which has caught media attention depends mainly on the testimony which came out under hypnosis. On August 17 1992 Gary Wood and Colin Wright were driving on the A70 towards Tarbrax when they encountered a classic 'flying saucer' hovering above the road. It was about 30 feet wide, stretching across both sides of the road and had a metallic sheen, with a dome or curve shaped upper section. Gary, who was driving and had been unnerved by the sight, 'put the foot down on the throttle' to rush below the object which hung about house height directly above the car. A shimmering curtain of light seemed to descend around them. Gary remembers next a period of blackness which seemed to last only seconds and then he was back in his blue Astra, the road before him, the UFO gone. He pumped petrol into the engine furiously and sped to his destination where he was taking a satellite television system. Colin and Gary found their friend's house in darkness. Knocking on the door they were amazed to learn that they had arrived at least an hour later than expected. They had set off at 10 p.m. It was now 12.45 a.m. the following morning. Their 30 minute journey had taken, inexplicably, five times as long.

After the encounter, Gary began to experience various unpleasant symptoms including headaches and bouts of extreme nervousness. He quickly connected these sensations to his strange vision on the A70. Having tried, but failed, to contact SEMR (which had changed address), he eventually found UFO investigator Malcolm Robinson who (according to *The Scotsman* newspaper) 'suggested hypnosis to try to account for the "missing time" on their journey'. It was a brave decision as BUFORA, of which Mr Robinson was Scottish representative, had long abandoned the practice because of the uncertainty of the testimony produced.

Following sessions with experienced hypnotherapist Helen Walters, details of an abduction by small grey extraterrestrials emerged. Gary described one of the 'greys' as having 'a translucent bone-shaped arm with long fingers'. While he was inside the spacecraft he saw a hole in the floor filled with fluid or some kind of thick, sticky material. As he looked, he saw 'a head appear out of it with a body and two arms. The creature must have been pretty big, bigger than me. It was like a skeleton with flesh around it. It had long arms, really long arms. It had a long body, really skinny, with the skin tight to the bone'.

He described the entity as having a large head with two prominent, but non-human shaped dark eyes. Its flesh appeared discoloured. These strange beings communicated with Gary using telepathy. Their purpose in abducting him appeared to be to carry out some form of examination. These remembered incidents were far from reassuring for either abductee, although Colin Wright seemed less concerned about the incident than his friend Gary. Indeed, Gary, he has said, continues to experience visits from alien beings, experiences which he finds of a disturbing nature.

The issue in all such cases is whether the abduction incident would have emerged without the patient being regressed. Can we be absolutely sure that the memory that emerged was a genuine recall or created through a fantasy of a thousand images collected from television, films, books and magazines? It is a long established fact that hypnosis can lead to witnesses recounting details that are manifestly incorrect. How do we separate fact from fiction? We are not dependent on hypnosis for abduction cases as there are plenty of witnesses worldwide who have conscious recall. False-memory syndrome may not be the answer in this case, but it has to be considered as a possible solution. It certainly cannot be the final word, because both witnesses are adamant about the strange craft which they came across and the time missing out of their lives. Neither witness contacted the police because they felt sure that the story would not have been believed. How do you start telling such a story, in any case? The delay in reporting it, however, meant that certain vital evidence was not examined. What, for example, happened to Gary's car during the period of the abduction? If they were lifted out of the car and put back in and at least an hour disappeared out of their lives, then that vehicle must have been stored or kept somewhere. If we remember Andrew Swan's strange experience and the effect that had on his car's electrical system, we can guess that in some way Gary's would have shown some indication that it too had experienced an 'abduction'. Unfortunately, however, the car was sold on and no testing or inspection was carried out. A real loss to ufology (and possibly mankind). One thing we can be absolutely sure about: something strange happened that night on the A70, but exactly what remains to be determined.

You don't have to be abducted by greys to have strange experiences. Brian Wilson's encounter while working in a pizza parlour has all the trappings of a farce, if it wasn't for sinister implications lurking just beneath the surface. Let Brian, a no nonsense individual, tell of the incident in his own words.

'In the summer of 1990', Brian explains, 'I was working as a full-time pizza chef in a chip/pizza shop in the New Town in Edinburgh. It was a busy shop, full of tourists who would come in for a home-made pizza. The pizza part of the shop was well decorated with a large display cabinet where most of the ingredients were kept, mushrooms, onions, peppers etc. We would make the pizza of the customer's choice there and then in front of them. Most customers found this exciting to watch as we would toss the pizza base in the air, pour on the tomato sauce and anything else they wanted on it. It was then put in the oven for a few minutes, then "hey presto!", you had your freshly made pizza. In the August of 1990 I was working with my colleague Doug the night that two rather small adults came in, about 5 feet in height. They both came and stood behind the counter facing me and with their right hands raised and their palms facing me announced that they were Americans. Their precise words were: "Hi, we're Americans". I thought this rather an odd thing to say as you can always tell Americans by their accents. Anyway, I said "Good evening, what would you like?" They asked me what we made and after I replied "pizzas" they turned to me and asked "What are pizzas?" My immediate thought was that it was almost unbelievable for a pair of Americans to not know what pizzas were. I looked at Doug with amazement and he was looking at me in the same way. I would like to add that during this brief time I had begun to think that they did look just a little bit strange. They were both rather small, the female had an odd shape to her shoulders, they were lopsided, and the male kept looking around the shop with a sort of amazement as if he had never been in a pizza parlour before. I did, though, begin to think that perhaps they genuinely did not know anything about pizzas. They then asked me to make up two pizzas. After I had put on the tomato sauce and cheese (which, by the way, they studied very closely) I asked them what toppings they would like. The female pointed to one of the containers and then asked what was in it. The container had green peppers in it and it was now that I started to think that they were either winding me up or had just landed from another planet. To not know what pizzas were was hard to swallow, but not being able to recognise a simple green pepper was beyond belief. Doug and I were looking at each other in disbelief and thinking that this was a big wind-up at our expense. The female asked if green peppers tasted nice, to which I replied "yes". They both wanted green peppers on their pizzas and they were then put in the oven to cook. During the few minutes their pizzas were in the oven I had to serve other customers who had come into the shop, but I did not notice anything unusual about them standing waiting, except that they stood perfectly still and did not say a word to each other. Their pizzas were ready and at last they paid me the £8 for their pizzas and I wished them goodnight as it was about 10.15 p.m. What was unusual when they left was that after paying £8 for two pizzas, they both took one bite out of the pizza they each had and threw the rest in the bucket outside the shop. I had read stories on the subject of alien life forms masquerading as human beings before and that generally they are not very good at doing so. I would certainly say that these two individuals came across acting as humans but also not doing a very good job of it. It was certainly very, very bizarre behaviour and although they did not make me feel threatened, they have left a very lasting impression on me.' Definitely a 'Strange But True' encounter!

I became involved in the next case through a mysterious phone call late one night. The caller told me of his own experiences, but also related strange happenings that involved a friend of his, David. He asked me if I was interested in finding out more, which I readily confirmed. He closed the conversation by affirming that if David was prepared to meet me he would get back in touch.

A week later the phone rang again. It was Andrew, my contact with the mysterious Dave. Dave had agreed to discuss his UFO encounters and so a meeting was arranged for the following Monday. That gloomy November evening found me parked at a run down shopping centre on Edinburgh's west side.

As I waited, the radio switched on, I realised with a shock that I had forgotten to ask my contact for a description. I had no idea what he looked like! Mentally I kicked myself for such a basic error. Dave knew I owned a grey Volvo, but I'd been forced to park in a dimly lit space beside a row of similarly dark coloured vehicles. If he didn't come to take a closer look he might easily miss me.

Cursing the cold, I killed the engine and following the pot holes made my way to the bus stop, our pre-arranged meeting place. A couple of men stood chatting to each other. A woman perched on the seat shivered in the cold. Since Dave had said nothing about a female presence, I suspected that the two blokes were the obvious candidates. As I considered an opening line, I grasped the unfortunate position I'd landed myself in. How do you introduce yourself to a stranger when you intend to have a conversation about UFOs? Would they view me as some weirdo and exact suitable revenge? I glanced at their faces and sized up their 'friendliness quotient'. I mulled over my opening lines like a playwright with his dialogue. Fortunately, the gods saved the day. A number 32 bus veered across the roundabout and grunted to a halt by my side. My anonymous chums shuffled forward and swung themselves aboard. Unless they suffered from an uncontrollable bus fetish, they clearly weren't my customers.

Then I heard voices. Real ones. I turned round and caught sight of three men in their late twenties chatting quietly to one another. They hadn't been there when I crossed the road, but must have come during my mental rehearsals. As I strove to catch their conversation, I noticed that the woman who had been at the stop shortly before had disappeared, though I hadn't seen her move or catch the '32'. I was beginning to feel as if I'd stepped into someone else's bad dream.

The spell, if that's what it was, was broken when I heard the words 'UFOs' and 'aliens' mentioned. Unless this was a bizarre coincidence this conspiratorial-sounding trio must be my intended contacts.

'Hi', I opened. 'I'm Ron Halliday. Are you Dave?' I'd guessed correctly and shook hands with all three, although I noticed that the large chap with blonde hair seemed a little less enthusiastic than the others. I put it down, at this stage, to a reserved nature, something I shared and understood.

We all crammed into my car and drove to Dave's flat, which turned out to be situated only a few hundred yards away. As I parked my car in a badly lit residents' square I was starting to feel a little bit uneasy. My efforts at conversation were met with a stilted response. The fair man seemed positively hostile. Was this all part of some huge set-up, with me as the victim? Was I being led up the garden path and a joke being played at my expense? The locks festooning the flat door, worthy of a Fort Worth gold vault, did nothing to allay my suspicions. Something odd was going on here. By now I was convinced of it, and gingerly tasted the herbal tea before taking a mouthful of the proffered liquid.

Sitting comfortably round the fireside, listening to Dave and his companions as their stories began to unravel, I started to relax. I continued to feel a shade tense, but was less sure of the cause. David had by now told of his own experience of seeing strange lights over Arthur's Seat in Edinburgh. But he was less concerned with his own encounters and much more interested in having his friend Gary tell me his incredible story.

Gary's problems began one October morning around 3 a.m. as he cycled on the track bordering the Union Canal. This ancient waterway had at one time connected Edinburgh and Glasgow before the Age of

Steam. It had long ago fallen into general disuse, but in recent years had been cleaned up and was a favourite run for small pleasure boats. For a good part of its length it is possible to walk or cycle alongside it and many people use it as a convenient route into the centre of Edinburgh. Gary, that morning, had turned onto it as a useful short cut to a friend's house.

The ninth of October was only a few hours old when Gary, pedalling quietly along, noticed a movement in the trees on the opposite side of the water. At first glance he thought it must be a street light which was probably being hidden by rhythmic swaying of branches caught by the breeze. Although he was trying hard to convince himself that the phenomenon was simply a natural effect, he found that he could not take his eyes away from it, staring at the spot in fascination.

Then his patience was rewarded. Over the tops of the trees arose a 'flying saucer', an apt description in this case, as it closely resembled the shape traditionally associated with UFOs. At the front, however, it carried what Gary could only describe as 'a spiky thing'. Beams of laser lights which looked solid in the dark? We can only speculate. The object itself appeared as large as a two storey house, plainly visible to anyone passing, undoubtedly solid and a kind of creamy beige colour.

Gary was, understandably, astounded and while he felt in no way threatened, he was cautious enough to mount his bike and head off in the opposite direction, pedalling furiously. As he glanced back he noticed that the object seemed to be following him, moving silently, close to the ground, its engine noiseless. Gary couldn't be sure how long the chase lasted, but when he turned off the canal-way at the first opening and looked back, the UFO was nowhere to be seen. Its sudden disappearance, however, did not end Gary's trauma. In fact, it was only the start.

Frightening incidents began to plague Gary's life. The phone would ring and a human sounding voice warn him to keep quiet about his encounter. Before Gary had a chance to reply the phone would go dead. On another occasion the radio in his livingroom started broadcasting, even though it hadn't been plugged into the socket. More disturbing still, strange creatures started appearing to him. Skinny aliens with large black eyes: the ubiquitous greys. Whenever they turned up, Gary would immediately feel paralysed and be unable to move. At one point the greys placed a device behind his ear and pressed what appeared to be a control button. A sharp pain coursed through his head. Instinctively, Gary knocked the device to the floor. The grey's response was far from friendly, snarling furiously and showing a row of unpleasantly sharp teeth. Gary was not physically harmed, but the message was clear enough. Whatever Gary wanted, his visitors were determined to have their own way. Over the following months the aliens (how else could they be described?) turned up at Gary's home at all hours. He could tell they had arrived by an unpleasant smell 'like rotten vegetables', which permeated every corner of the room. Even when he moved to a friend's house for temporary refuge, he couldn't escape their attention. One visited him there.

By now Gary was beginning to wonder if his imagination had detached itself from his conscious control. In short, was he still sane? To test himself, the next time a grey appeared he reached out his hand to touch its arm. If it was solid he would know that this was no figment of his imagination. As he stretched his arm forward, his visitor immediately seemed to sense his intention and, showing an incredible strength which belied its puny frame, firmly, but gently pushed Gary's hand away. The alien showed no resentment at Gary's clumsy gesture, and instead warned him to keep clear of Arthur's Seat, a hill which, as I have pointed out on numerous occasions, may hold the key to many of Edinburgh's mysteries. The grey then disappeared. By the time I spoke to Gary, the visits had come to an end though the thought of them still caused him visible concern. Gary's experience may not be unique in the history of ufology, but it is certainly unique in Scotland.

Gary's experience reflects an established tradition in human/alien contact. The unsuspecting witness who, minding his own business, suddenly finds himself confronted by extraterrestrial intelligence.

But can we go one stage further? Is it possible to argue that alien beings are amongst us and may even have married into our species, producing hybrid offspring? The idea may challenge the beliefs even of those who have soaked themselves for a long while in the lore of ufology, but, again, I would draw attention to the experiences of people who have confronted this possibility. They are straightforward, sensible people with no axe to grind and no personal gain. Their only 'reward' may be to suffer the indignity of laughter and derision. It is unfortunate that individuals who have experienced strange incidents feel a reluctance to come forward. Society has a lot to learn from what they have been through. I have permission to tell one particular story, but, to safeguard the people involved, I have changed names and places so that identification is not possible. The substance of their experiences, however, is as it is told.

June had her first UFO experience when she was ten, at her home in Craigmillar, Edinburgh. She can't be sure of the exact date, but believes it was during 1963 at the height of the 'Beatles' fame. June was sleeping in bed but woke with a start. Outside her window she caught sight of a very bright white object moving slowly. It seemed to be getting closer and closer, growing in size. Interested rather than frightened, June called to her father to come and see. He, however, could see nothing out of the ordinary in his daughter's sighting and told her it was only 'a big bright star'. How like a father! Typically, no sooner had he closed the bedroom door behind him, than the object which was now eye-shaped, started moving towards the window again. Eventually, and June can't remember which, the mystery light either disappeared, or she went to sleep!

June can't recall any strange incidents in her teens, but after she was married she experienced a most strange recall. She visited the Island of Barra, situated in the Outer Hebrides, while on holiday. It was her first trip to the site, but during her stay she became convinced that she had lived there previously. She seemed to know the place so well and recalled incidents that had occurred in her past. June's husband became disconcerted by his wife's familiarity with the island. He knew they were both strangers to Barra and could not understand her conviction that it was well known to her. So strong did June's feeling become of her previous existence on the island that her husband became quite concerned and then even frightened by the implications of June's knowledge. June's reaction was quite the opposite. She felt elated because, as she says, 'she had come home'.

June's life was blighted by tragedy in 1982 when her husband was killed in a car crash, leaving her to bring up her family on her own. The night after the accident, her daughter Laurie came running to June, begging her to come and see a 'big star'. The large white object in the night sky seemed to be blinking directly at them. There was no doubt that they felt it was a sign from heaven. The children said 'goodnight' to the star and then it vanished.

The series of strange incidents which intruded on June's life continued the year after she was widowed, during a family holiday to Hull with her brother. Their route took them across an area of moorland, June is not sure exactly where, and because it was a clear night they stopped to watch the stars. It was then that the inexplicable happened. One of the stars started to move and get closer. This so unnerved her brother, who had always been afraid of the dark, that he insisted on getting back into the car and leaving the spot immediately, in spite of June reassuring him 'they won't harm you'. Then, out of the blue, a police car appeared. Neither June nor her brother had caught sight of any headlights or heard the sound of an approaching vehicle. A policeman stepped out and came over to June asking what they were doing. She replied that they had stopped for a minute and were on their way to Hull. He asked them to follow him off the moor and they drove along behind till both cars came to a crossroads. The policeman indicated they should turn right, which they did, and he turned left. When they turned back it was as if the police car had vanished into thin air.

Nineteen eighty five was to be the year of strange events. June returned to Barra for a second visit and sensed again that she was 'coming home'. One day during this visit she went down to the beach and saw the figure of a man, standing alone. She immediately felt that this was her dead husband, John. June walked towards John and as she did so everything around her went quiet, even the breaking waves. She was now within a few feet of her husband and only at this point did she realise that it was not John. Had June mistaken a complete stranger for a man she had lived with for years? This might be an obvious conclusion except that she heard this mysterious figure say, 'I'm very sorry that I'm not who you think I am, but everything will be okay'.

June was so upset by these words that she fell to her knees and felt herself being lifted back to her feet by an invisible force. She glanced round to check on the children, and when she looked back the strange figure had disappeared. The incident was so remarkable that it was used in a sermon broadcast on BBC Radio Scotland.

For several years afterwards, things were relatively quiet. Then, in 1991, events began to gather pace. In October of that year, June's older daughter was playing at her friend's house. It was situated only a few hundred yards away, but meant walking through an area of wooded parkland, so June decided to walk over and pick her up. By this time, it was evening, but an evening with a different air about it. The lights in June's house were fooling about, flickering and generally misbehaving. The video recorder would switch itself on and off. The electrical fault, if that's what it was, started with the lights in the living room, travelled to the video, then moved on to the microwave in the kitchen. It was all a mystery to June and anyway there was Linda to pick up.

On her way back, part of the way through the wooded area, June became aware of a bright blue light. It shone so strongly it hurt her eyes and every so often as the wind gusted the area beyond the light became visible. And there it was. A solid object hovering (or standing) amongst the trees. And although strong wind blew, there was no noise whatsoever. June was frightened. She was shouting at it to go away, saying in her head that she had to get home. Then in the blink of an eye the UFO had gone. June was more than relieved. She was convinced that the object had wanted to take both her and her daughter. But if that was true, what on earth had frightened it off?

In 1991, June met Ruth. It was a significant event. She felt that she had known Ruth all her life. It was this relationship with Ruth that would open June's eyes to the reality of extraterrestrial contact. Ruth, June learned, had had a miscarriage, but conceived again nineteen days after the tragic incident. Both women felt that these two events were related, but in a way most people would find difficult to accept. For Ruth and June are convinced that Ruth's husband Leonard is either in part or wholly alien. Their child, Christopher, is therefore a hybrid belonging both to the earth and a planet beyond our galaxy.

Let me assure the reader that this account has not deliberately stepped into the realms of science fiction. These are the facts as related to me by those involved. Is intermarriage between 'aliens' and humankind such an illogical idea? Are there really 'aliens' or other beings who are not really so different from us? Entities who can walk and talk amongst us and so parallel our own behaviour that we would not recognise them as 'ET'? Yet, if you looked and watched closely, you might note some differences not discernible to the casual observer.

Leonard, I am told, seems at times translucent. He talks very little. He moves slowly. He has no close friends. He works in a top secret military base.

If Leonard has this odd air, then why on earth (if you'll excuse the expression) did Ruth marry him? It seems, at least according to June, that Leonard singled Ruth out, almost as if he was hunting her down. A strange story starts to hang together. An entity not from this planet seeking a mate, not at all for sinister reasons. Had we been put on planet X, would we not do exactly the same?

Following her marriage, Ruth moved to a west coast city. Soon afterwards she experienced odd goings on in their new home. Lights started to flicker, dim and go out. Electrical appliances would switch themselves on and off.

One day Christopher, then 18 months old, went missing. Somehow he had clambered out of his cot and across Ruth without waking her. Just as Ruth woke up and discovered he was gone, Christopher walked back into the room. His eyes were red, almost as if something had been done to them. After this incident Christopher was extremely agitated and Ruth asked June to come through and visit her. Both women had already noticed that June had a calming effect on Christopher. Was it something to do with the fact that both she and the child were fascinated by the sight of the stars?

During a stay at Ruth's house an incident occurred which convinced June that she really was involved in a case of alien contact. She woke up one night and found herself sitting, freezing cold, on the edge of the bed.

She recalled seeing a bright light shining at the rear of Ruth's house with the whole kitchen lit up. She had gone down to the kitchen and caught sight of a white figure standing at the breakfast bar. Its aura glowed forcefully and the impression conveyed to June was one of sheer beauty. The figure was of human height reaching June's chest. June says she is five feet nine inches tall, so the being she saw must have been at least five feet. Slowly she (June was convinced she was female) reached up and put her hand on June's shoulder.

'Everything is going to be all right as you are a guardian', she told June. At this point, June woke up.

Was this incident the beginning or part of an abduction sequence? In some ways it does fit the pattern. To June, however, the fact of her and Christopher's contact with alien intelligences are incontrovertible. Several times both she and Christopher have woken in bed with muddy feet, proof that they have been led away by alien entities. And if, as Ruth believes, Christopher may have been implanted in her, isn't it likely that this race might wish to have contact with one of their progeny? As June points out, ancient civilisations too were obsessed with the stars. Is that a clue to our origins? June is convinced of two facts. Aliens 'walk the earth just like we do'. Every night before she goes to bed June goes into the garden and looks to the skies as 'she knows they are out there'.

If alien beings can contact us, shouldn't it be possible for us to contact them? Of course, there are many individuals who will come forward with claims to have met and talked with extraterrestrials. There are few, however, who can show you such a being. Perhaps there is only one such person. There is certainly only one in Scotland. His name is Alex and he wishes no publicity, on the sensible line that no-one will believe it even if they can see what he can do. And if I were to add that what Alex does is to show you the *spirits* of past aliens (as well as humans) then you will realise just how incredible this story is. It really is beyond belief. Unless you have seen these faces. Sitting in Alex's living room, in full light, people have reported several different types of non human entities. Spirits of our ancestors also appear. It seems the earth is being given a message. Humans and aliens are all part of one vast universal family, but we cannot count forever on the toleration of those from outside this planet. From what is reported, it appears that these beings have no bad will towards us and that in the land beyond we will all come together as one. The universe is both vast and small. Earth has its place, but Mankind is by no means alone.

EIGHT

SCOTLAND'S UFOs - AN ENIGMA

Are Scotland's UFOs any different from those witnessed in the rest of the world? Is there anything distinct about the UFO phenomenon in Scotland? These are the type of questions investigators should be asking if they want to determine the reality or otherwise of the phenomenon. Of course, some would argue that the sheer volume of the reports is convincing proof in itself that 'something strange' is taking place in Scottish and the world's skies. Others would also argue that the number of abduction cases, particularly in the United States, must lead to the inescapable conclusion that we really are being visited by alien beings from another civilisation. On both counts I would urge a note of caution. Steuart Campbell in his book reviewing the photographic evidence for the Loch Ness 'monster' has shown that the sheer number of snaps of Nessie do not prove its existence. If we take each alleged photograph on its own merits, then the evidence disappears because each individual photograph does not stand up to scrutiny. Are UFO reports in the same league?

My own concerns centre on the substantial difference between the volume of reported abduction cases alleged in the USA compared with the British Isles. I do not have accurate figures (if there are any) but to state that there are at least 100 such reported cases per million of population in the US would certainly not be an overestimate. In Scotland that would give us a comparative 500 cases and in England over 2,000. Yet in Scotland we are talking about a handful - a couple of dozen possibly - reported incidents. There are not many more than that reported from England. So are we really suggesting that aliens find Americans more worthwhile to abduct than English or Scots or other Europeans? It is an anomaly and one that can't easily be explained or wished away. I write this more in puzzlement that in a wish to downplay the experience of abductees or those who have encountered alien entities. The experiences for these individuals are too real, frightening and baffling to dismiss. I believe that such people have seen something that is not imagination or hallucination, but on the other hand does not fit easily into the ET hypothesis. Are these really beings from a distant planet, light years away from Earth? For centuries people have experienced encounters with strange beings. I am reluctant to accept such experiences as myth and ET as simply a 'modern myth'. Eye witness testimony may be suspect, but vast areas of life are ruled by the reality of what we as human beings see and experience. Why should seemingly bizarre encounters be dismissed simply because they do not fit the rules of a world order that we ourselves have established? Perhaps our picture of the universe should be redrawn in a less fixed and certain manner.

Yet, it does seem to me largely true that the vast majority of UFO reports are explicable as natural phenomena. One evening in October 1996, for example, I received a number of telephone calls from the town of Irvine on Scotland's west coast. The callers told me basically the same story. A big light shaped like a spoked wheel was clearly visible in the sky. The UFO had been hovering in the same spot for two hours and looked big, larger even than the full moon. The urgent tone of these witnesses excited me and I urged them all to video, photograph or draw the object for later analysis. Could this, I wondered, be the evidence ufologists had been looking for?

Irvine was too far away for me to get to that evening, so I immediately rang Air Traffic Control at Prestwick Airport. This transatlantic stopover is only a few miles from where the spoke shaped UFO was being seen. ATC were well aware of the excitement as they had been swamped by anxious residents worried by the appearance of the strange object. They were in touch with the police who were, even as we spoke, investigating the incident. They suggested I call back after 10 p.m. when the air flight path would be quieter and we could discuss the matter further. When I rang back the incident had been solved. A nightclub, the 'Aquarian' (how apt!) had bought a powerful spotlight and the new gadget was projecting an image onto the clouds. Our UFO! The police had asked them to turn it off and the town had gone quiet. Much to the relief of Prestwick Airport! An understandable mistake for the townsfolk, who quickly forgot about it, but an incident of longer term concern for ufologists.

That odd light was an unusual object for the witnesses, but what are we to make of 'less excusable' reports? Venus is regularly misidentified as a mysterious object. Perfectly sincere, rational individuals have videoed it believing they have caught something weird on film. Why? The fact that individuals do report Venus or Sirius or Mars as a UFO undoubtedly fuels the scepticism of those who would dismiss the whole business as nonsense. Clearly, when people see Venus as an alien spaceship, they may well be seeking to create mystery out of nothing. This doesn't detract from the evidence of those who have had a close encounter or witnessed lights behaving in strange ways. It does, however, urge us all to be cautious. A mysterious light in the sky could be all sorts of things, or nothing. Do we create a mystery by the simple process of investigating it? No UFO investigator should be frightened by declaring a UFO to be an IFO (an Identified Flying Object). It enhances rather than reduces UFO research if it can be shown that ufology is about real and not imagined mysteries.

However, at the end of the day, if we go through all the likely explanations for what a strange light might be and discover that none of the obvious explanations fit, for example civil aircraft, planets etc, what exactly are we left with? The problem is that we are left with nothing in particular, to be exact. All we have is an unidentified object - not an alien spacecraft. Given that the vast majority of UFO sightings consist of 'lights in the sky', are we talking about a phenomenon of any significance whatsoever? Isn't this as David Clarke and Andy Roberts argued in their book *Phantoms of the Sky* simply a 'modern myth'? A fantasy projection of our twentieth century minds? A twentieth century folk tale 'developed to combat our fear that we are alone in the Universe'? Today we see UFOs, three hundred years past it would have been witches on broomsticks and fairies, or something allegedly equally unlikely.

This argument, any reasonable person would have to accept, has some substance to it. Given that no alien spaceship has landed in Glasgow's George Square or Edinburgh's Princes Street or outside the White House, where is our proof? Pointing to thousands of sightings of lights flashing or hovering in the sky doesn't, I would suggest, undermine the case of sceptics. Frankly, sceptics don't worry me too much, but it is of concern that the evidence to counterbalance their scepticism does seem on the surface weak. And it is weak because the nature of the evidence does not come across as scientific and science is extremely important in the twentieth century in deciding the viability or otherwise of a point of view. Of course, it is not the whole cake, otherwise religion and spirituality would be consigned to the proverbial 'rubbish bin of history'. They haven't been. On the contrary, they are growing, and thus eye witness accounts and a person's belief that he has experienced something strange still count for something. You may not convert science's materialist outlook, but you may change the minds of others.

Some readers may be puzzled at this point. They may ask, 'Do we really need to rely on eyewitness accounts? What of the physical evidence? Traces on the ground? Photographs? Bits and pieces of extraterrestrial crafts? Surely there is enough of this type of evidence to back up whatever has been recorded by the naked eye'. Obviously UFO encounters are a world wide phenomenon. I don't want to state the obvious, but sometimes we overlook the obvious. If we remember that UFOs are global, then we can also realise that over the last fifty years there have been many tens of thousands of UFO sightings. In Scotland alone there are over a thousand documented cases out of a population of only five million, with many more seen but not recorded. Yet out of all these incidents, how many encounters have left behind definite scientifically provable traces? How many nuts-and-bolts from interstellar space craft do we find littering our highways and byways? As much as any UFO investigator I dream of finding that piece of metal which definitely is not of earthly origin. In 1993 I thought I had got lucky.

One afternoon I received a phone call from Ian Kyle, then of the *Edinburgh Evening News*. A walker on Dechmont Law had discovered a strange metallic tube. It was about a foot high, a few inches in diameter, with a gold coloured base. It looked as if it had been badly burned. The object had been taken to the police station in the nearby town of Livingston where it was being kept under lock and key by George Martindale, the station custodian. The police had no idea what the object was. It was something completely out of the ordinary. They had asked around, but everyone seemed baffled and could offer no solution.

So now the question was, 'Could it have come from a UFO?' The object had been found on Dechmont Law, not too far from where Bob Taylor had experienced his 1979 encounter. There had been sightings in the area over the years, so the possibility did not seem too far fetched. In the United States, for example, there had been many claims that whole spacecraft had been locked away in secret hangers. Was it so unlikely that in Scotland a piece of the galactic jigsaw would turn up by chance? At the time, put on the spot, I suggested taking it to the nearest university laboratory where it could be properly examined. If it was made of unknown materials then its non-terrestrial origins would quickly emerge.

The story with my comments appeared in the papers the next day, accompanied by a photograph of the object, which looked unremarkable. However, it had been associated with UFOs and, therefore, had been cloaked in an aura of mystery. The mystery soon evaporated. That night I received a call from a local Roman Catholic priest. He had seen the story and recognised the object. It was an incense burner stolen from the church the previous week. He was delighted to get it back and sorry he had spoiled a good story. The sceptics had a field day.

I would make it clear that I am not deriding all alleged physical evidence, only urging an ever sounding note of caution. Supposed parts of spacecraft have tended not to stand up to scrutiny. They may not have been disproved, but they do not provide substantial evidence. I would agree that there are interesting eyewitness accounts of secret machines tested far from the prying eyes of the public. I too have heard reports of mysterious goings-on at Machrihanish. On several occasions I have been in receipt of phone calls from an individual who has claimed to have documented evidence that 'alien craft' were stored and tested at that West Coast base. I even arranged a meeting in Glasgow, to which my mystery caller did not turn up. The evidence that alien technology has been tested and flown over Scotland may well be in existence, but so far it has not emerged into the public arena.

Have we been more successful with other aspects of physical evidence? Several cases have occurred in Scotland where strange objects have been seen on or near the ground. There are other incidents where odd markings have been discovered on their own or in conjunction with bright or unexplained lights. Have these encounters left evidence that might provide proof of extraterrestrial contact? The Bob Taylor incident once again provides a good example of the kind of problems faced when dealing with evidence of this nature. At the site of Bob's encounter there were both ladder type impressions in the ground and circular marks. This seemed to corroborate his account in so far as it provided proof that a solid object of some type had been in the vicinity. However, was this object one that would shatter the sceptic's view of ufology? Steuart Campbell's response was that the markings could be explained by engineering or other equipment that had been left in the area at a recent date. It could not be proved conclusively, but there was no doubt that official groups had been active in the woods during this period. The depressions left on the ground could certainly have been produced by equipment left overnight or longer. As any gardener knows, marks can be visible on grass for a considerable time after they have been made. So it is an open verdict on whether the marks that were investigated could be linked to the craft seen by Mr Taylor.

Unfortunately, other incidents associated with physical evidence have in all probability not been so thoroughly examined. The evidence is not significant. Where soil or wood samples have been analysed by SEMR, the results have been inconclusive with no confirmation that any unsuspected chemical or molecular change has occurred. The results of the 1976 Elgin case are not available, but if they had proved to be significant I dare say that they would be public knowledge by now.

Some enthusiasts have pointed to the occurrence of crop circles as proof that flying saucers have landed. This evidence is less enthusiastically promoted than it was a decade ago, but it still has some supporters. The crop circle debate has been an extensive one and it is not my intention to enter into it. However, crop circles have appeared in Scotland and so some comment is relevant.

As far as Scotland is concerned, there is not a great deal to link crop circles with UFO sightings. A major problem is that there have been so few circles in Scotland compared with the south of England. A worrying aspect, perhaps, if we accept the reality of crop circle incidents. Of the few circles that have been known about none can be definitely linked to a UFO sighting. It is true that circles have appeared in the general area of UFO activity, as at Blairgowrie (one time 'UFO capital'), and at Corpach beside Fort William. However, so many areas experience UFO incidents that the proximity of a crop circle is statistically a near certainty, I would suggest. It is interesting that West Lothian with its hundreds of UFO reports has only one known crop circle - at the side of Linlithgow Loch in 1992.

But do we need physical evidence to prove that witnesses have genuine UFO experiences? It may be that these experiences do not involve solid objects. One suggestion has been that powerful emissions of electro-magnetic energy might stimulate individual perceptions and so allow individuals to see into other dimensions. This would explain why a particular witness might experience a strong and vivid incident that another person might be completely unaware of. Returning to the Bob Taylor sighting, electro-magnetic stimulation would account for the fact that whilst the object he saw appeared perfectly solid over most of its parts, sections of it appeared translucent so that Bob could see through it. Bob, in effect, caught sight of an object that was part in and part out of our dimension. If we recall also Pat Macleod's encounter on a busy Edinburgh road, or Tom Coventry's sighting in Glasgow, both in broad daylight, both it would have been thought easily visible to others, then the electro-magnetic explanation does provide an answer. The stimulation is on the individual and thus the UFO sighting is really limited to that one person. Multiple witness sightings might be explained by the strength of the stimulation which at certain times in certain areas might affect individuals in a wider area. Some have argued that there is no need to add inter-dimensional viewing as an explanation. The Electro-magnetic stimulation simply produces a type of sensory hallucination. It does appear to be the case that laboratory tests can stimulate paranormal type experiences. But simply because an experience can be simulated in a laboratory, does that nullify the experience of the witness in the field? I don't think so, because one problem with the electro-magnetic explanation is its ability to focus on an individual rather than a crowd. Can it be argued that electro-magnetic energy can focus itself so readily? It does seem unlikely. Although in its favour it is undoubtedly true that certain areas experience many more sightings than others and it might well be linked to unexplained concentrations of electro-magnetic activity.

If strange lights in the sky do not provide substantial evidence, can we so readily dismiss the close up encounters? Let's leave aside the abduction cases for the moment. What can we say to incidents like those of Pat Macleod's where the sighting of the object is perilously close. Perilously close for scientists and sceptics, I mean. Those who pour scorn on UFO sightings adopt two basic attitudes to these types of close encounters: the witness is either deliberately lying or otherwise he or she imagined it; the 'mirage of Venus' scenario put forward by Steuart Campbell. If you adopt this response to the subject then no matter the incident you will always have an explanation. For example, Steuart Campbell can explain away Pat Macleod's sighting as yet another mirage - the planet Mercury on this occasion! There is an attempt in such cases to put forward any scientific sounding explanation which may provide a solution even where the solution seems more unlikely than the incident. I have no idea what Pat Macleod saw, but I don't believe it was a mirage of Mercury . Nor do I believe that Bob Taylor's encounter was a mirage of Venus, an epileptic fit or ball lightning. If sceptics feel more comfortable that they have 'solved' incidents in this way, then so be it. UFO investigators should happily leave them to it and get on with the real work of exploring the unknown. Whatever rationalists and sceptics might say, or argue, unexplained phenomena will continue to occur because there are incidents which simply cannot be explained.

Unfortunately, with abduction cases we enter a difficult world (in several senses). Having spoken to those involved in these cases, I know only too well just how severely individuals can be affected by these experiences. The last thing these people need is to be derided or have their sanity questioned. This is particularly true in Scotland where the number of abduction cases will always be relatively small because of the limited population. Yet many of the stories related by Scottish abductees correspond to accounts given by abductees from other parts of the world. Are we dealing here with a global alien phenomenon? Possibly, but on the other hand the use of hypnosis and the many portrayals of alien contact on screen make it difficult to determine where fact and fiction begin and end. Sceptics will have none of it and dismiss it all as fantasy. UFO researcher Malcolm Robinson stated that he had become convinced of the reality of alien contact through his involvement with one particular case, the alleged abduction incident on the A70 (see Chapter 7). However, is a witness's sincere conviction that he or she has been abducted evidence of the reality of the phenomenon? Should we accept an individual's claims simply because of repeated assertions that they are true? If hypnosis is the sole evidence that we have, are we bound to accept its results as proven facts? It's a question that it's hard to give a definite answer to because each person is different and our acceptance of an account may vary according to our own judgement of the individual concerned. I accept through my own research that we have difficult incidents to explain, but it is a leap from that to argue that we are being visited by aliens from another planet. I have no truck with those who simply put it down to a modern myth, but my own feeling is that we are dealing here with an area that might be more complex than the proverbial 'men from Mars'. Surely there are advanced civilisations and those who have found ways to turn light years into mere inches of travel, just as we now orbit the world at a speed unbelievable even a hundred years ago. On the other hand, can we be so sure about the material nature of our world and the heavens around it. What do we really perceive? Is our knowledge, perhaps, limited by our own human senses and beyond those senses lies another world which we can rarely, but sometimes do, experience? By nature I'm inclined to both possibilities, but whatever answer we eventually find or whether we continue searching for ever, I am sure that there is far more to life in the universe than we have even started to dream about.

There are individuals even in Scotland who claim that there is nothing unusual about abduction incidents as they are regularly 'abducted' and in contact with alien intelligence. According to *The Sun* newspaper Graham Wyllie from Dundee set up a 'telephone helpline to counsel people claiming to have been kidnapped by invaders from space'. Mr Wyllie had, it seems, undergone such an experience, having been 'kidnapped by a friendly alien called Josef'. He expressed the view that there might well be an invasion and take over by alien 'greys' of the Earth and this would come about when a certain proportion of the Earth's population had met the aliens. Mr Wyllie might be correct. I can't claim to have spoken to any aliens, but I suspect that any extraterrestrial beings who are capable of visiting the Earth and kidnapping individuals would have little trouble in taking over the whole planet. A galactic war involving Earth and ET hardly seems a viable option.

There are so many channellers of alien messages that it has become hard to know exactly which messenger is relaying an accurate message. They can't all be right. If there are genuine messages and true mediums through which this information is being conveyed then their letters are being swamped by an unfortunate pile of junk mail. Let us hope that the urgent fax eventually gets through.

In recent years individuals have gained world wide attention with their views on alien intelligence. These ideas are often well thought out, eloquently expressed and completely different.

David Icke, in his book "*... and the truth shall set you free*", expounds his belief that there are many extraterrestrial intelligent life forms. For many millennia, he claims, the Earth has been trapped in a shroud of what he calls "negative vibrations" that cut Man off from his higher self and prevent him reaching his full potential, both as an individual and as a race. This, he says, is the result of an intergalactic battle between negative and positive extraterrestrial intelligences where, at present, the negatives are in the ascendant, at least in this quadrant of the Universe. These negatives feed off the negative energy our misery produces. They have controlled the Earth to produce war, famine, plague and death through the machinations of their stooges, a global elite (whose main focus is the United States, but which also includes highly placed politicians, business executives and international agency members throughout the world) which they, themselves, control.

The positives, centred in the Pleiades, are now on the verge of making a breakthrough, and, with the help of increasing positive thinking from an ever expanding number of people and organisations, they may be on the verge of a breakthrough.

Icke produces a powerful and convincing body of evidence to support this viewpoint.

Zecharia Sitchin's thesis is very different (although the two viewpoints are not, in fact, mutually exclusive). A scholar of ancient languages, Sitchin describes in his book *Genesis Revisited - has modern science caught up with ancient knowledge?* how the story of Earth's origins and the birth of Man as told in 6,000 year old Sumerian texts are being confirmed by modern scientific research.

The Sumerians described the solar system as having 12 'planets' - the sun, moon and 10 planets. In modern times the ninth planet, Pluto, was only rediscovered in 1930. The tenth planet, called Nibiru by the Sumerians and Marduk by the Babylonians, was pulled into the solar system from outer space by the sun's gravity and entered an elliptical, retrograde orbit round the sun that took 3,600 years to complete. This caused it to crash into the planet Tiamat, then in the orbit of the asteroid belt, splitting it, knocking half of it into a new orbit where it became Earth, and the remaining shattered fragments became the asteroid belt. Modern data gleaned from space exploration now confirms much of this story and many astronomers have become convinced that there is indeed a tenth planet.

The Sumerians tell how the Annunaki, the technologically advanced people who had evolved on Nibiru, came in their spaceships to Earth about 5 million years ago to mine for gold. They developed slaves called 'adams' to work the mines for them. These 'adams' were made in the first instance by a process of in vitro fertilisation and surrogate motherhood, using eggs from the apemen (or rather women) who had developed on Earth and Annunaki sperm. This hybrid was initially infertile, but became fertile after DNA manipulation. Modern DNA research tends to support this theory.

Mr Sitchin completes his book with the fascinating hypothesis that the Annunaki, who seem to have been fairly quiescent for many millennia, are returning to our orbit. The loss of Phobos 2, sent to investigate Mars, and other clues from anomalous factors in Martian photographs, appears to indicate that they may have reactivated their ancient space base on that planet, and don't want us to know about it ....

The author's scholarly knowledge of ancient languages and wide ranging information on current research gives his book a powerful credence. He is not tied to the micro-view of academic researchers, but is able to take a macro-view of many disparate strands, ranging from medicine, linguistics, astronomy, biochemistry and archaeology to religion, to produce his shattering, but convincing, thesis.

Scientists, of course, have been divided about the possibilities of life existing elsewhere in the universe. The American astronomer Francis Drake examined the possibility that advanced civilisations might be found on other planets. Using various calculations, he concluded that there might exist in our own galaxy alone many 'earths' capable of supporting life and potentially developing the technology to achieve interstellar travel. Sir Arnold Wolfendale, former Astronomer Royal and President of the Institute of Physics told a conference at Stirling University that he did 'believe there were intelligent beings somewhere else in space'. He explained, 'I think there is life out there, but it is less common than people think ... The distances are incredible and I think that means that the chances of getting visitors are pretty small'. Sir Arnold also made the point that it was far more likely that alien civilisations would attempt to contact us by radio first rather than attempt to visit us. Of course, it might be argued that aliens would do it their way rather than the way we might predict!

Attempts by the European Union, according to *The Scotsman* newspaper, 'to set up an observatory in France to search for UFOs' sparked a storm of protest from British politicians. Sir Teddy Taylor, a Conservative MP with anti-European Union views, declared it 'a madcap venture'. He was concerned that there were 'a lot of MEPs who are rushing around Europe asking people whether they have seen a flying saucer ... The whole idea seems to have been cooked up in some kind of ethereal dream world', and he was particularly concerned that they were studying the 'extent of aliens taking control of areas of outer space around the world'. He described this as 'the biggest piece of nonsense I have ever heard in my life!' In response to Sir Teddy *The Scotsman* published an article I wrote which pointed out that many government and military establishments, including those in France, Russia, the US and Britain, had been interested in UFO sightings for many years. I concluded, 'Many people have now claimed to have seen something in the sky which they cannot explain. Europe has recognised that the UFO phenomenon requires investigating. Is that really an outlandish objective?' Surely the interest shown by the governments of various countries and by their military is evidence that UFOs are not at all 'phantoms of the sky', but genuinely inexplicable phenomena. When, for example, conversations of the following nature occur, aren't we, the public, entitled to wonder what is going on, and to receive some explanation?

Glasgow Air Traffic Control (ATC): "Cleared to land."
Pilot: "Has somebody just taken off?" (Urgent tone in voice.)
ATC: "No. Why?"
Pilot: "Some lights are oscillating at the end of the runway, going back and forth, oscillating fairly rapidly."
ATC: "OK. We'll check it out. Where exactly is it?"
Pilot: "It's half, or one, mile from the end of the runway, oscillating rapidly. One dot either side of the runway centreline."
ATC: "OK, we'll make sure and check it out."
Pilot: "It's very strange indeed." (Obvious puzzlement in voice.)

The incident took place on 26 February 1996 at 7.18 p.m. In spite of our enquiries, no explanation has been forthcoming.

There has been in recent years a considerable amount of video footage taken in Scotland, including UFOs caught by Margaret Ross in Stenhousemuir, Barry McDonald in Falkirk, the Malcolm family in Lanark and several others. Much of this video footage has been of excellent quality, yet no matter how good the video evidence, it will always be suspect in the eyes of sceptics. We still want the one hundred per cent convincing piece. It may, of course, never come. If UFOs are really intelligently guided extraterrestrial craft then, presumably, they will be seen when they want to be and not before. Unless, of course, one crashes. Mysterious balls of light crashing into the ground have been seen on many occasions in Scotland, but without any evidence of a metallic craft being involved. There are plenty of military areas within Scotland where a 'spacecraft' could be stored, but in spite of numerous sightings, associated particularly with Machrihanish, we await disclosure from anyone who worked there.

Naturally, in this kaleidoscope of views and claims, the more outrageous the story the better attention it grabs. Reports from channelling centres the world over would fill a section on its own.

Those who hold to the view that we on Earth really are alone were shaken by claims that life might have existed on Mars, claims made by respected scientists. This controversy arose because of impressions of primitive organisms found in rocks in Antarctica: rocks, it was argued, which had arrived from Mars. Hard on the heels of this discovery came the discovery of a large planet, about the size of Jupiter, orbiting the unimaginatively titled HR3522 star in the constellation of Cancer, 40 or more light years from Earth. Neither of these finds proves that extraterrestrials are visiting Earth or even that advanced life forms exist elsewhere in space, but it is a reminder that we cannot be certain that we are the only life forms in the Universe. Chance would surely point to the existence of many planetary civilisations and if they are out there, wouldn't they share with the inhabitants of Earth a wish to find sister and brother lifeforms? If the Universe is one whole entity, then we must all, surely, be driven by the same inner force. To seek and find anyone, wherever they are, whatever they are, who shares this vast inexhaustible space we call our own.

WHERE TO CONTACT: FURTHER INFORMATION

If you have had a UFO experience or video footage or photographic evidence you would like to report, please write to Ron Halliday, Scottish Earth Mysteries Research, 35 Fountain Road, Bridge of Allan FK9 4AU, Scotland.

Scottish Earth Mysteries Research produces the quarterly magazine *Phenomenal News* edited by Viv Alexander. For information about subscriptions or to submit aticles, contact Viv Alexander at 4 Linden Avenue, Stirling FK7 7PG.

SEMR in conjunction with 'Jolly Good Productions' has produced a video called *Unknown Scotland* (£7.50 including P&P). Available from either SEMR or 'Jolly Good Productions', 18 Kingsfield, Linlithgow EH49 7SJ

FURTHER READING

Very little has been published about Scotland's UFOs. In every sense *UFOs: The Scottish Dimension* respresents the fruits of primary investigation. Recent years have seen the production of a variety of Scottish UFO magazines. First of these was *Enigmas*, which I started with Malcolm Robinson in 1989. It ceased publication in 1996. *Phenomenal News* published by Scottish Earth Mysteries Research is now Scotland's foremost UFO magazine. David Colman has produced much interesting material in *Cover-Up*. Otherwise, Scottish UFO incidents have appeared mainly in the newspapers and various English based UFO and paranormal magazines.

Allingham, Cedric:	*Flying Saucers From Mars*, London, Muller (1954).
Andys, Eris	'Northern Lights', *Fortean Times,* Issue 81 (1995)
Arnold, Kenneth and Palmer, Ray	*The Coming of the Saucers* (1952)
Campbell, Steuart	'Close Encounters at Livingston', *Case History No 1*, BUFORA (1982)
Campbell, Steuart	*The UFO Mystery Solved*, Edinburgh, Explicit (1994)
Clarke, David and Roberts, Andy	*Phantoms of the Sky*', London, Robert Hale (1990)
Daniken, Erich Von	*Return to the Stars*, London, Corgi (1972)
Devereux, Paul	*Earth Lights,* Wellingborough, Turnstone (1982)
Evans, Hilary	*UFOs 1947-1987* London, *Fortean Times* (1987)
Halliday, Ron	*Mysteries of the Scottish Landscape*, Bridge of Allan, Aura (1988)
Halliday, Ron	'The Bonnybridge Phenomenon', *New Ufologist* Issue 6(1997)
Halliday, Ron	'Bonnybridge Bites Back', *Northern UFO News* No 164 (1994)
Hynek, J	*The UFO Experience*, London, Corgi, (1974)
Keel, John	*UFOs: Operation Trojan Horse*, London, Souvenir (1970)

Leslie, Desmond and Adamski, George	*Flying Saucers Have Landed*, London, Werner Laurie (1953)
Mantle, Philip and Nagaitis, Carl	*Without Consent*, London, Ringpull (1994)
Oakensen, Elsie	*One Step Beyond*, London, Regency Press (1996)
Pope, Nick	*Open Skies, Closed Minds*, London, Simon and Schuster (1996)
Randles, Jenny	*Strange But True*, London, Piatkus (1994)
Randles, Jenny	*The Paranormal Year, 1993*, London, Robert Hale (1993)
Randles, Jenny	*Abductions*, London, Robert Hale (1988)
Randles, Jenny	*UFO Retrievals*, London, Blandford, (1995)
Randles, Jenny	*Star Children*, London, Robert Hale, (1994)
Robinson, Malcolm	'The Fife Incident', *Sightings* (1996)
Robinson, Malcolm	'Central Scotland in Grip of UFO Wave', *Enigmas* (Feb/March 1993)
Robinson, Malcolm	'UFOs: The Study Goes On', *Enigmas* (May/June 1993)
Robinson, Malcolm	'Japanese Film Crew Probe Bonnybridge Mystery', *Enigmas* (August/Sept 1993)

Index

Index

N

O

P

Q

R

S

Index

T

U

W